Taos Hiking Guide

Taos Hiking Guide

by Cindy Brown

NIGHTHAWK PRESS
TAOS, NEW MEXICO

Author: Cindy Brown
Cover photo: Cabresto Lake by Cindy Brown
Photos: Cindy Brown, unless otherwise noted
GPS data: Cindy Brown
Maps: Dharma Maps, www.dharmamaps.com
Graphic design: Wink Visual Arts, www.winkvisualarts.com
Copy editing: Matrika Word Services
Published and distributed by: Nighthawk Press, Taos, New Mexico

FIRST EDITION 2019
Fifth Printing

Library of Congress Control Number: 2015940221

ISBN: 978-0-9862706-2-8

To my parents, Barbara and Les Brown,
for their love of nature

Table of Contents

HIKES

Acknowledgements

Thank you to the team that helped make this book a reality: publisher Rebecca Lenzini of Nighthawk Press, copy editor Laura Lynch of Matrika Word Services, and designer Kelly Pasholk of Wink Visual Arts. Thanks to Carol Terry for her review. Appreciation goes out to Ginny Williams, Kim Van Deman, and Doug Scott of Taos who first suggested that a hiking book was a good idea. Thanks to Steve Tapia for his book on wildlife and for being a fellow journeyer on this path. Special thanks to Joan Livingston at *The Taos News* for the opportunity to write a hiking column and for her permission to use the material for this book. I appreciate the dedicated staff at the Carson National Forest and the Bureau of Land Management for their timely responses to my many questions, and the members of local hiking clubs who have shared their expertise. Local merchants Taos Mountain Outfitters, Mudd-n-Flood, and Cottam's have contributed so much to the hiking columns and the book. And thanks to Marc at Dharma Maps for his expertise and excellent maps. Thank you to Kay Matthews, author of *Day Hikes in the Taos Area,* for allowing me to contribute to the final edition of her classic book. Finally, thanks to everyone who has been hiking with me, braving snow, thunder, lightning, bears, and more, including Joe, Sawyer, Carol, Erica, Damaso, Pat and Anna Lena, Bob, Dennis and Dog, Coral, Lou, Carlos, Jo, Claudia, Kathy, Betsey, Willa, Steve, Steph and Ben, Brenda, Weston, Amanda, Mike, Justin, and Reefka.

REGIONAL MAP

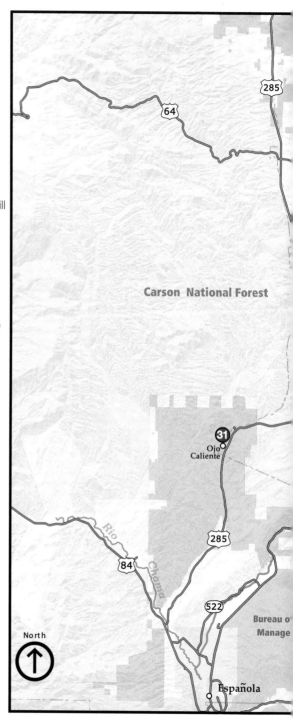

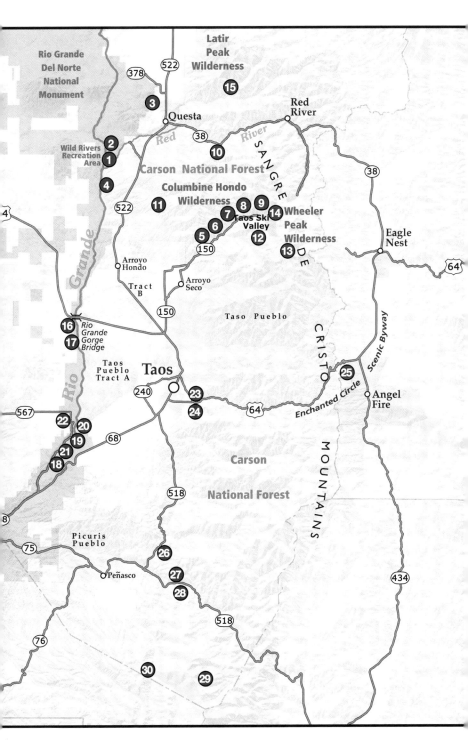

TABLE OF HIKES

#	HIKE NAME	LAND	CNF#	DIFFICULTY
1	Little Arsenic	BLM		Moderate
2	Big Arsenic	BLM		Moderate
3	Las Vistas de Questa	BLM		Moderate
4	Cebolla Mesa	CNF	102	Moderate
5	Yerba Canyon	CNF	61	Moderate - Difficul
6	Manzanita Canyon	CNF	58	Moderate - Difficul
7	Italianos Canyon	CNF	59	Moderate - Difficul
8	Gavilan	CNF	60	Moderate - Difficul
9	Long Canyon to Gold Hill	CNF	63/64	Moderate - Difficul
10	Columbine Canyon	CNF	71	Moderate - Difficul
11	San Cristobal Canyon	CNF	78	Moderate - Difficul
12	Williams Lake	CNF	62	Moderate
13	Wheeler Peak	CNF	67	Difficult
14	Bull-of-the-Woods	CNF	90	Moderate
15	Lake Fork to Heart Lake	CNF	82	Moderate - Difficul
16	Rio Grande West Rim - North	BLM		Easy
17	Rio Grande West Rim - South	BLM		Easy
18	La Senda del Medio	BLM		Easy - Moderate
19	Rift Valley	BLM		Easy - Moderate
20	The Slide Trail	BLM		Moderate
21	Picuris	BLM		Moderate - Difficul
22	La Vista Verde	BLM		Easy
23	Devisadero	CNF	108	Moderate
24	South Boundary	CNF	164	Moderate
25	Elliott Barker	CNF	1	Moderate
26	Amole Canyon	CNF	10/182	Moderate
27	Canon Tio Maes	CNF	5	Moderate - Difficul
28	Comales Canyon	CNF	22	Moderate - Difficul
29	Serpent Lake	CNF	19	Moderate
30	Santa Barbara	CNF	24/25	Moderate
31	Posi Pueblo	BLM		Easy - Moderate

BLM = Bureau of Land Management
CNF = Carson National Forest

ROUND TRIP	ELEVATION IN FEET		
	START	END	DIFFERENCE
2 miles	7,500	6,740	760
2 - 3 miles	7,500	6,800	700
3 - 14 miles	7,600	8,200	600
2.6 miles	7,300	6,300	1,000
7.8 - 8.6 miles	8,200	11,800 - 12,115	3,600 - 3,915
8.4 - 8.6 miles	8,400	12,000 - 12,115	3,600 - 3,715
7.4 - 10 miles	8,600	11,500 - 12,115	2,900 - 3,515
5 miles	9,000	11,800	2,800
9 miles	9,400	12,700	3,300
12 miles	8,000	11,800	3,800
9 miles	8,500	11,600	3,100
4 miles	10,200	11,040	840
10 miles	10,200	13,161	2,961
4 miles	9,400	10,900	1,500
9 miles	9,200	11,500	2,300
3 - 18 miles	6,900	6,900	0
3 - 18 miles	6,800	6,800	0
5 miles	6,000	6,000	0
3 - 6 miles	7,000	6,800	200
2.6 miles	6,100	6,800	700
1.5 miles	6,100	6,700	600
2.5 miles	6,400	6,400	0
5 miles	7,200	8,304	1,104
3 miles	7,200	8,200	1,000
6 - 8 miles	8,500	9,500	1,000
4 miles	8,300	9,300	1,000
4 miles	8,300	9,300	1,000
8 miles	8,200	10,700	2,500
7 miles	10,300	11,800	2,500
6 - 8 miles	8,900	9,700	800
2 miles	6,000	6,380	380

Introduction

Welcome to hiking in Taos!

Whether you are new to town or interested in exploring new areas, this guide will help you find great hikes at all levels of difficulty and in all directions from Taos. The hike descriptions originally appeared as monthly hiking columns for *The Taos News*. Thanks to managing editor, Joan Livingston, for her permission to share these hikes with you.

Taos is a place of incredible natural beauty. If you are lucky enough to live here or to be visiting, you can experience that beauty by hiking the nearby trails. Sunny days make hiking possible year-round, and each season has its special beauty. Many of the trails are lightly traveled, especially those in wilderness areas. While exploring the Sangre de Cristo Mountains, you may get to experience glorious views of lakes and peaks in perfect quiet and solitude. While hiking near the Rio Grande, you may see messages from ancient peoples who passed near the river in the form of rock carvings, known as petroglyphs. Although we don't always understand the symbols, we feel the presence of the past.

PETROGLYPHS

TAOS MOUNTAIN IN THE MIST

Being in nature soothes the spirit and can also boost energy and creativity and even improve concentration and focus, according to many recent studies. Nature provides the opportunity for solitude, as well as meaningful connection with family and friends. Time spent outdoors allows us to experience the senses. We are part of the wilderness, just like the blue columbine, the red-tailed hawk and the coyote. In the fall, we see the trees quaking in the wind – wearing their golden leaf party dresses – before the long quiet sleep of winter. On an early summer morning, we can feel the cool dampness of the mountain canyon in the morning near the creek, after the rain. We can touch the undisturbed spider web from the night that tells us that we are the first people to pass this way today. We can sit at the lake, in a moment of calm and silence. We remember the life of the body, not just the mind.

TAOS

Taos is located in Northern New Mexico, just 40 miles south of the Colorado border. One-and-a-half million acres of Carson National Forest and 656,000 acres of Bureau of Land Management land surround Taos. Hiking is found on desert mesas near the Rio Grande, as well as in the surrounding Sangre de Cristo Mountains, where elevations exceed 12,000 feet and trails climb above the tree line. Taos Mountain is on Taos Pueblo and not accessible to the public.

All the hikes in this book are located within a 45-mile radius of Taos and are easily reached usually by paved roads. Where the access includes dirt roads or requires a four-wheel drive vehicle, these conditions are noted in the directions section of the hike description.

HOW TO USE THIS GUIDE

At the beginning of the book, you'll find recommendations for what types of gear and clothing you will need, depending on the season. There is information about wildlife – what to see and how to react, as well as tips on reducing your impact on nature and trail etiquette. Also included is some information about snowshoeing.

The guide is divided into sections to help you find the hikes nearest you. Each hike description starts with information on the length, level of difficulty, elevations, and highlights of the trail, to help you choose which hike is right for you. The book is light enough to carry in your backpack, or you can make a copy of the hike you are planning to try. Read on for ideas on how to get out in nature, see beauty and stay safe.

EXPLANATION OF DIFFICULTY RATING

The trails in this book are rated for level of difficulty, so that you can assess which hikes are right for you. If you want to scan the hikes by difficulty, take a look at the table that is found after the regional map. Here is a brief overview of what the designations mean:

EASY usually signifies a hike that is relatively flat, with a trail in good condition. The easy hikes are typically closer to Taos and don't require a four-wheel drive vehicle to reach.

MODERATE means a trail that has some more steepness. Trails that are moderate in difficulty, but are quite long or in more remote areas will include notes about the more challenging nature of the hike. You will see that many of the trails are designated as moderate in the lower sections, but rated as more difficult as you move to higher elevations.

DIFFICULT indicates that the hike is among the more challenging options in the area. It may climb to high altitudes, above tree line, making it very important to observe weather patterns, so that you don't get caught in a lightning storm on an exposed ridge or mountaintop. Trail conditions can include steep and rocky sections. Difficult hikes include very long trails and those that go to some of the tallest peaks in New Mexico. None of the hikes in this book require climbing gear.

TIME ESTIMATES

Estimates of time to complete the hike are given for some of the longer hikes. Usually the time indicates how long the trail takes if hiking briskly. Add additional time for slower hiking and for breaks taken.

Preparations

GETTING STARTED

It is important to note that Taos is a dry, semi-arid place located at almost 7,000 feet above sea level, and many of the hikes in the area take you above 12,000 feet.

You might choose to start your hiking in Taos by visiting:

- **Taos Visitor Center** is on the south side of town at 1139 Paseo del Pueblo Sur, tel.: (575) 758-3873. There is a room devoted to hiking trails and maps, and the people at the desk can answer your questions about the current weather patterns.

- **Carson National Forest** has an office at 208 Cruz Alta Road, tel.: (575) 758-6200; a good source for trail conditions on national forest land.

- **Bureau of Land Management** (BLM) Taos Field office is located at 226 Cruz Alta Road, tel.: (575) 758-8851. This office is a good resource for planning hikes on BLM land.

Alternatively, you might visit one of the outfitters to pick up a few supplies or pieces of equipment and get some advice about current conditions. See a complete listing in Appendix A – Resources.

QUESTIONS TO ASK

As a visitor or a newcomer to the area, you might ask yourself:

Am I coming from sea level or low altitude?
If coming from lower altitude, it is wise to choose a flatter hike to begin. Many of the visitors to the area that come from sea level or low altitude locations find that the higher altitude causes them to be short of breath at times and to tire more easily. You may notice your mouth, eyes, and lips are drier than usual and you require more water to stay hydrated.

What is my usual level of physical activity?
If you are regularly active, you may experience fewer problems hiking at higher altitudes. Consider your fitness level, along with that of the other people with you, as you plan your activities.

How much time do I have here?
If you have moved to Taos or are going to be in town for several days, you may have the chance to gradually work up to more difficult hikes.

What is the weather like?
Sometimes a pattern of clear mornings and stormy afternoons develops during the summer. You may want to plan your hike so that you finish before mid-afternoon. It might be surprising to hear that people get hypothermia, even in the

summer, because they are caught in a cold rain or snowstorm at higher elevations. Also be aware that the wind can pick up suddenly and cause the temperature to feel much colder, especially as you reach higher areas and mountaintops and ridges. See the sections that follow for more detail about weather during different times of year.

ALTITUDE

Altitude sickness or Acute Mountain Sickness can affect anyone starting at altitudes above 6,500 feet, including people in good shape. Strenuous exercise can aggravate altitude sickness. Although not common, the altitude can cause serious problems that have sent some visitors to the emergency room.

Signs of altitude sickness:

• Headache

• Fatigue

• Stomach upset

• Sleep disturbances

• Dizziness

Remedies:

• Drink lots of water, 6 to 8 glasses a day.

• Use a product like Altitude Adjustment to add drops of electrolyte replacement to water.

• Rest your first day here or if you feel any signs.

• Limit sugar, as it can be dehydrating.

• Herbs like ginseng support the adrenal glands to combat stress on the body.

Doctors recommend that you spend a day or two becoming acclimated before attempting something strenuous like a steep hike. Of course, if you have any known medical conditions related to the heart or breathing, you will want to consult your doctor. Also be wary of hiking in couples where one hiker is in better condition or more ambitious than the other. I find that the most successful way to ensure an enjoyable hike is to let the slower hiker lead, setting a steady pace that can be maintained for an extended period of time.

When hiking in a new area, especially at altitudes beyond what you are used to, it makes sense to hike with at least one other person. On an uphill hike, you may want to rest every 10 minutes to avoid becoming suddenly overtired. It is always a good idea to let someone know where you will be and when you will be back.

HYPOTHERMIA

Hypothermia can occur when a person is exposed to wet, cold, or windy conditions. The body loses heat – faster than it can generate it. As body temperature drops, the heart, lungs and other body systems cannot function properly. If not addressed, hypothermia can lead to death.

The signs of hypothermia include: shivering, dizziness, disorientation, hunger or nausea, trouble speaking, loss of coordination, fatigue and fast heartbeat. If anyone in your group experiences signs of hypothermia, it is important to move them into shelter, away from cold and wind. If clothes are wet, they should be removed and the person covered with blankets or warmed slowly with a fire. If the symptoms become severe, seek emergency medical treatment as quickly as possible.

Hypothermia can be avoided by bringing layers of warm clothes and being aware of impending storms. If a rain or snowstorm moves in to the area, return to lower elevations. Although it is hard to give up a day of hiking or a peak you hoped to reach, it is better to stay safe and healthy and try again another day.

HIKING GROUPS

There are a variety of informal hiking groups in Taos. Check with local outfitters for contact information.

CHECKLIST FOR CLOTHING AND EQUIPMENT

One of the great joys of hiking is that it doesn't require much equipment to get started. A good pair of hiking boots is the most important thing you'll need. As you become more experienced, you will begin to identify simple pieces of equipment that can add to your enjoyment. Here is a list of basic clothing and gear:

TO WEAR:

- Sturdy, waterproof boots
- Wool socks
- Layers of clothing that can be removed and replaced easily, including a waterproof outer layer
- Hat for the sun
- Sunglasses

TO BRING:

THE BASICS:

- Water – Carry your own water for day hikes in water bottles or a reservoir like Camel-bak.
- Food – Trail mix, energy bars, and nuts are easy to carry.
- Sunscreen and lip protection – Local outfitters have non-toxic products.
- Rain jacket
- First aid kit
- Bug repellant – for summer
- Compass – Bring one even if you have a GPS; it can malfunction.
- Map or hiking book
- Bandana
- Knife
- Matches
- Flashlight
- Whistle

NICE TO HAVE:

- Electrolytes in powder or liquid form
- Arnica in gel, cream, or pill form to take if injured to help reduce severity
- Field guide on flowers, birds, mushrooms or other areas of interest
- Camera
- Binoculars
- Poles – Helpful for crossing streams and climbing steeper sections

FOR LONGER HIKES IN MORE REMOTE AREAS, CONSIDER:

- Bear repellant – A fogging spray that is effective up to 40 feet away
- Small folded emergency blanket

SPECIAL CONSIDERATIONS FOR WINTER HIKING

CLOTHING:

- Layer clothing that can be removed as the day grows warmer
  - Base layer in silk or synthetic material
  - Warm layer in fleece
  - Wind-proof and water-proof coat or shell
  - Gaiters or water-resistant pants
- Warm hat or headband and gloves
- Traction device. Consider bringing a traction device (like Yaktrax or micro-spikes) that straps on your boots.

Hiking requires considerably less investment in clothing and gear than some other winter sports. However, the key to comfort is several layers of the right stuff. You can start with some basic clothing and add additional pieces later. First, the base layer: choose a wool, silk, or synthetic fabric. Kim Van Deman at Taos Mountain Outfitters explains, "The first layer needs to wick away moisture from your skin. I like merino wool the best; it works with your body so you don't get that chilled feeling when you stop."

As a second layer, something warm like a fleece sweater or another wool piece is a good choice. The final layer should be a wind-proof and water-proof shell. Even if you don't expect to encounter wind or snow, it is important to wear or bring this layer as the weather can change quickly. A wind pant or a pair of waterproof gaiters over your boots will help keep out wind and moisture. Layers are important because you will create heat while walking uphill, but you don't want to sweat, as that can cause you to feel cold later. Carrying some layers in your backpack while you are headed uphill allows you to add a piece when going down.

Hat, gloves, and something to protect your neck and face are the final pieces of a good layering system. A scarf or neck gaiter to cover up the gaps that can be left by zip-up pullovers and coats helps to reduce drafts. Sunglasses are a must to reduce the glare of the sun on the snow.

What to Expect on the Trail

WILDLIFE

As you hike near Taos, you may see some amazing wildlife. Elk and mule deer are among the more commonly seen animals, especially as you gain altitude and come into the open meadow areas. You might see bighorn sheep both in the Taos Ski Valley area and also along the Rio Grande, where a herd was recently introduced. The blue grouse, a large pheasant-like bird, is also seen frequently, especially in the lower canyons near water.

BIGHORN SHEEP

SNAKES

Although you won't often see them, there are snakes in both the desert-like environment near the Rio Grande and also near wet creek areas. You are most likely to spot garter snakes or even the colorful smooth green snake. The only poisonous snake in this area is the rattlesnake – identifiable by its brown and white diamond pattern and rattle. The bull snake can look similar and imitate the rattlesnake by hissing. While not poisonous, this snake can inflict a painful bite and is best avoided. If you see any snakes on the trail, you can back up and let the snake escape – that will likely be the end of your encounter.

MOUNTAIN LION AND BLACK BEAR

Less commonly seen animals include mountain lions and black bear. Although these animals are only seen occasionally, be aware of your surroundings and notice areas of disturbances like trees with claw marks or rocks that have been overturned by bears looking for ants. You can also be on the lookout for paw prints and animal droppings or scat. Most animals are anxious to avoid humans and will generally try to stay out of your way. The black bears in this area eat berries and insects. They are most commonly seen near trails during the fall. Francisco Cortez, the local wildlife biologist with the Forest Service, reminds us that fall is when bears are trying to fatten up for the winter. Due to summer drought conditions some years, there may not be enough berries, acorns, and other food for the bears, and thus are on the move looking for new sources of food.

Whenever you are in the wilderness, it makes sense to keep children and pets close to you and to make noise as you hike, especially if there is background sound from water running or wind blowing that might mask your approach. If you encounter signs of animal activity, including a deer kill, you may want to leave the area. It is important never to approach any wildlife, as doing so may trigger a defensive attack, especially if there are young animals with adults. Matt Pengelly, Taos Game Warden for the New Mexico Department of Game and Fish, says that black bears are the only ones we see near Taos – even if their fur is almost white, brown, or black. These bears are generally non-aggressive. Pengelly says that it is "extremely rare for a black bear to attack a person." He says it is important to give the bear some space and most often the bear will move off the trail. "It is best not to surprise them; make some noise, let the bear know you are there," says Pengelly.

HERE'S A SUMMARY OF WHAT TO DO IF YOU SEE A BEAR OR MOUNTAIN LION ON THE TRAIL:

- Do not block the path of travel or escape route.
- Do not run – predators can outrun humans.
- Back up slowly and speak in a firm voice.
- Make yourself look larger by waving your arms or a stick.
- If attacked, fight back, and if someone in your group is attacked, help them fight back. Use your hiking poles or stick to defend yourself or others.

In my time hiking in Taos over the course of more than 25 years, I've seen flocks of wild turkeys, herds of deer and bighorn sheep, coyotes, bears, and snakes on the trail, along with an amazing variety of birds, including bald eagles and golden eagles. In all cases, I was able to observe the animals and give them room to escape, before I continued on the trail. Seeing wildlife is a rare experience and one of the things that makes hiking in nature so memorable and special. In New Mexico, it would be very unusual to have a violent encounter with a wild creature, so don't let fear keep you off the trails!

WEATHER AND PLACES TO HIKE

SUMMER

Often a sunny morning is followed by a stormy afternoon during the summer, especially after the monsoon season begins, usually in July. You may want to plan your hike so that you finish before mid-afternoon. Surprisingly, people get hypothermia, even in the summer, because they are caught in a cold rain or snowstorm at higher elevations. Wind can pick up suddenly and cause the temperature to feel much colder, especially as you reach higher areas and mountaintops and ridges. You may encounter snow on some of the higher trails during the summer months. If you begin your hike in the early morning or end it in the early evening, be aware that wildlife is most active during these times of the day.

Even the sunniest morning can be followed by a stormy afternoon. Watch for signs of dark clouds moving in. In case of heavy rain, lightning, or hail, move to lower elevations and take shelter in densely forested areas.

Although weather is a consideration, summer is a good time to explore the mountainous areas that are less accessible in the winter, including the Wheeler and Latir Peak Wilderness, as well as the Columbine Hondo Wilderness Area and the hikes southeast of Taos, reached by NM 518, such as Serpent Lake.

SPRING/FALL

RIO GRANDE NEAR WILD RIVERS

If you live in Taos, you know that during the spring or fall, it can be 70 degrees and breezy one day and snowing the next. It makes sense to pack some waterproof and windproof outerwear and to dress in layers that can be easily removed and carried with you. You may also wish to wear a hat for protection from the sun and elements.

There might be snow on some of the trails well into May and June. Snowmelt causes the creeks to rise, which may be a consideration, especially if you are planning a hike along a creek, like those found on the Ski Valley Road. It is always a good idea to talk to someone living in the area about the current trail conditions.

In the fall, aspens turn yellow in late September and early October, depending on the elevations. The hikes along NM 518, including Amole Canyon and Santa Barbara near Peñasco, are good places to look for turning aspens.

WINTER

Although winter hiking requires more thought and preparation, there are so many unique pleasures that the extra work is worth it. The trails are quieter, offering more opportunities for peace, silence, and views of wildlife. Near Taos, there are trails with a little snow and those with lots of snow, so there are many choices. If you want to keep hiking through the winter months, here are some things to consider.

Preparation: One important way to make outdoor winter activities more enjoyable is to eat a good breakfast before setting out. Some of us are tempted to grab a quick bite and head out to the trail, but we could find ourselves out of calories and more vulnerable to the draining effects of the cold. As Chris Pieper of Mudd-n-Flood says, "Have some more butter on your toast. Saturated fat keeps you warm."

Hikes with less snow: Although conditions will vary, the hikes near the Rio Grande tend to get less snow and more sun. So while there might be some snow and slush, the trails are usually easier to hike. The west rim of the Rio Grande can be reached from the rest area, just west of the Rio Grande Gorge Bridge on US 64. This flat trail is 9 miles long and goes all the way south to join the trails in the Orilla Verde recreation area. Surrounded by sage, this trail is a good place to see sage sparrows nesting in the brush or bald eagles soaring up and down the gorge. Deer and elk can sometimes be seen by the river in the gorge. Another trail system near the Rio Grande is found north of Questa at the

CLIFF WITH SNOW

Wild Rivers area. A variety of hikes follow some moderate switchbacks down to the river. Just east of town in Taos Canyon, the Devisadero trail offers another good choice for those looking for a sunny hike. A steady climb through some rocky sections brings you up high enough for good views back into town.

More snow: A variety of spectacular trails along creeks are accessed from the Ski Valley Road, including Yerba and Italianos Canyon. Some sort of traction devices and poles are recommended for the creek crossings, which can be icy at times. After a new snow, parking along the side of the road can be more challenging, as the plows move the snow off the road and onto the shoulders, usually used for parking.

Staying safe: Before setting out, check in with the local outfitters or resources to get the latest information on conditions. Certain trails may have avalanche risk, as the snow gets deeper. Always let someone know where you will be and when you are expected back.

Chris at Mudd-n-Flood says, "If you are new to Taos, never let yourself breathe too hard. At sea level you can recover. But here, if you exert yourself too much, you'll find it much more difficult." He adds, "You'll get a workout, but you are at altitude and need to respect that. Give yourself enough time; be prepared, relax and enjoy."

SNOWSHOEING

When the snow gets too deep and you start to step through the crust, also known as *post-holing*, it is time to get out the snowshoes.

The Williams Lake hike is great for snowshoeing. It begins at over 10,000 feet in elevation at Taos Ski Valley. The road to the parking lot on Deer Lane requires a four-wheel drive vehicle during the winter months. It is also possible to park at the base area and catch a ride with the shuttle up to the trailhead. Signs pointing the way to the trail have been added, making it easier to navigate around the Phoenix Grill and up to the trailhead, although a stop at the hot chocolate and espresso shack is worth a slight detour. One advantage of recreating at Williams Lake is that there are more amenities here than are available at most trailheads. In addition to the coffee shack and the Phoenix Grill, the Bavarian restaurant is located near the trailhead and provides a good place to start or end the day.

The trail begins up a wide section along the Rio Hondo, where hikers share the road with skiers and snowboarders returning to the chairlift. The trail moves into the woods and follows a series of switchbacks. Then the forest opens to the left, revealing some slide shoots on the steep mountainside. After returning to the woods for a moderate uphill climb, views open to the right across the boulder fields that are often buried deep in the snow during the winter months. Finally, there is one more short uphill section, before reaching the lake. It is a 2-mile trek that is considered moderately difficult in the summer. But the added work involved in navigating the snow, especially in snowshoes, requires more exertion and even the "I-live-at-altitude" locals may find they have to stop to catch their breath on the ascent. It might generally take about an hour to cover the 2 miles to the lake, but in the winter, allow a bit more time for the uphill section. Although this is a popular trail, there is still the opportunity for solitude, especially around the lake.

Additional options: Other trails for snowshoeing near the ski valley include Bull-of-the-Woods, accessed from the base area parking. The Southwest Nordic Center has a yurt for rent, located near the 2-mile mark on Bull-of-the-Woods. There is a wood burning stove and space for up to 10 people. To reserve the yurt, contact Southwest Nordic Center at (575) 758-4761 or go to the website at www.soutwestnordiccenter.com for information.

Kathy De Lucas, Public Affairs Officer with the Carson National Forest, recommends Forest Road 437, near Valle Escondido for snowshoeing. The forest roads are closed from the end of December until May, making them pleasant for hiking. Another favorite for snowshoeing and other winter activities is Amole Canyon, south of town off NM 518, just about 30 minutes from downtown. To check conditions, call the Carson National Forest at (575) 758-6200 or stop by the field office at 208 Cruz Alta Road.

Wildlife: Bighorn sheep are attracted to bare hillsides where the snow has melted or been blown away. Other big game animals often move to lower elevations to find food. Many predators such as bobcat and coyotes will follow the big game. The snowshoe hare might be spotted in areas of deep snow, as the shape of their paws allows them to stay on the top of the snow and run quickly from predators. Birds such as the mountain bluebird, Steller's jay, and nuthatch can be heard and seen in the forest.

Tours: Here are a few long-standing tour operations and winter recreation areas. You can check with Taos Visitor Center for additional options.

Stuart Wilde with **Taos Snowshoe Adventures** says that when he leads groups on snowshoes in the winter, they often see tracks and other signs of animals. He says, "We may not see a big herd, but we see the tracks of mule deer, elk, bobcat, and coyote." Wilde offers tours for beginners, as well as more advanced snowshoers. He says family groups can tour together. He has a sled to pull small children. One advantage of being part of a tour is that you may find yourself on some lesser-known trails. Wilde says, "As a guide, it is my job to find the good snow." When asked what people like best, Wilde says that it's the solitude, "feeling like we are the only group out in the woods." To find out about current tours, call (800) 758-5262 or visit www. snowshoetaos.com.

Northside at Taos Ski Valley also offers guided snowshoe tours. Daytime adventures include 2-mile hikes on private land. A shuttle from the base area to the trailhead is provided, along with snacks and water. Full moon touring is also offered. Rental equipment is provided when needed. Call for more information and reservations (575) 776-3233 or visit www.ridenorthside.com.

YERBA CANYON CREEK CROSSING

Enchanted Forest Cross Country Ski Area offers snowshoeing on flatter terrain and has staff to provide assistance. In business for three decades, Enchanted Forest has 18 kilometers of marked trails in the Carson National Forest. For more information, visit www.enchantedforestxc.com or call (575) 754-6112.

Gear: Taos Mountain Outfitters has snowshoes for sale; you can reach them at (575) 758-9292. Mudd-n-Flood on Bent Street has snowshoes for rent and sale as well as other winter gear; try them at (575) 751-9100. Cottam's Ski Shops has snowshoes available for rent at their midtown and ski valley locations; call either (575) 758-2822 or (575) 776-8719.

BEST ADVICE ON BEING OUTDOORS IN THE WINTER:

"Have the right equipment with you. Stay hydrated and well fueled. Don't overdress, but be prepared. Wool is great."

— Kim Van Deman, Taos Mountain Outfitters

"For clothing, think warm and dry, but not bulky. The scenery is gorgeous when the sun shines on the snow on the mountains."

— Ray Valerio, Cottam's Ski Shop

GETTING LOST

Although most of the trails in this guide are well-marked, there are some sections that are less traveled and may be harder to follow. Here are a few suggestions that may help keep you from getting lost.

Prepare: Before you set out for the hike, read about it in a trail book, check a map, or do some research online. Both the Carson National Forest and the Bureau of Land Management have good websites that include trail descriptions for many of the hikes.

Tell someone where you are going: Let someone know when you are expected back and at what point they should call and report that you are missing. Check in with your contact person when you return.

Map: Take a map with you. Copy or print out a map and carry it with you.

GPS: If you have a GPS system or have an application on your phone, start it up at the trailhead. If you are going for a very long hike, you may want to carry a lightweight charger, as use of the GPS on the phone does draw down your phone battery. GPS helps track your route, how long you've been hiking and how far you've come. If you wander off the main path and feel unsure of how to proceed, you can look at your route on GPS and head back toward what looks like the point you left the main trail.

Compass: If you have a GPS, you may want to carry a compass as well. A compass is very useful in combination with a map to ensure that you are headed in the right direction.

Even with preparation and the use of these tools, you may become lost from time to time. It is important to stay calm, stop, consult your maps and GPS, and then make a plan. If you are able to get re-oriented to your position, you should be able to make your way back toward the trailhead. It is important to carry extra food and water, in case you are out on the trail longer than expected.

If you become lost or someone in your group has not returned on time, either dial 911 or call the Taos County Sheriff at (575) 758-2216 or the New Mexico State Police at (575) 758-8878.

HIKING ETIQUETTE

Many of the trails allow horseback riders and some allow bicycles and off-road vehicles. Here are some guidelines:

Uphill Hiker: It is customary to yield the trail right of way to the uphill hiker, so that he or she can maintain momentum going up.

Groups: If you are in a group that is moving more slowly than a hiker or group in back of you, please step to the side and let the faster moving hikers pass you.

Horseback Riders: If there are horseback riders on the trail, step off and let them pass.

Bicyclists: Bicyclists should yield to hikers, but be on the lookout as you may have to get off the trail to accommodate bicyclists, if they don't yield to you.

HIKING WITH CHILDREN

Introducing children to nature through hikes in the woods is a great way to ensure a lifelong love of being outside. At the same time, be aware that children may have less stamina than adults and less interest in walking long distances. You may want to review the table of hikes and choose a trail in the "easy" category to try first. Although wildlife around Taos is typically not a threat to humans, keep children close by in order to better keep them safe, if wildlife does appear. Monitor children for signs of altitude sickness, and remember that if they become too tired, you may be carrying them all the way down the trail. Be sure to bring extra food and water and allow additional time for children to explore the trail at their own pace.

DOGS

In Taos, many people hike with their dogs. Although most experts recommend that dogs remain on leash, you will find that not everyone follows that advice.

If you encounter a dog off-leash, stay back and give the dog room to go around you. Don't approach an unknown dog, but if the dog approaches you, talk casually in a friendly tone. There is a deterrent spray favored by bicyclists and joggers called HALT that can be used on aggressive animals and is less dangerous to them than pepper spray or Mace.

HERE ARE THE LAWS THAT APPLY:

Carson National Forest (CNF): According to the Public Affairs officer at the CNF, there is no federal law regulating dogs on national forest land. She says, "We strongly recommend that dogs stay on leash or under voice command. They can chase wildlife and may get injured themselves when they encounter a hoof or claw." She notes that not all people like dogs and they should be able to hike without the threat of unwanted dog interactions.

Bureau of Land Management (BLM): At BLM developed campgrounds, picnic areas, and trailheads, dogs are required to be on leash. Most of these areas are posted with signs that remind owners of the rules. In less developed BLM areas, owners may chose to let their dogs off-leash, but owners are still responsible to make sure that dogs don't harass wildlife, people or other dogs. Owners are asked to pick up after their dog on the trails, and the 'pack-it-in, pack-it-out' rule applies to dogs, as well as people.

Town of Taos: All dogs must be on leash in town and town-owned parks. In Kit Carson Park, "mutt mitts" and trashcans are provided, and owners should pick up after their dogs. There is now a small off-leash area at Kit Carson Park. Another exception to the leash rule is the dog park located near Stray Hearts Animal Shelter. Dogs over 4 months old may come to the park, where they are required to be off-leash. A current rabies tag and a free tag issued by Stray Hearts are necessary, and male dogs must be neutered. The dog park is located at 1200 Francis Lane, off Salazar near the bypass and is open from 8 a.m. to dark daily.

Taos County: Dogs off their own property in Taos County must be on a leash and have current rabies vaccinations.

TRADITIONAL USES

Much of the Carson National Forest and Bureau of Land Management areas were used for wood and piñon nut gathering, grazing, fishing, hunting and trapping before the land became public open lands. These uses continue and are regulated through permits and other means. Hunting is allowed on much of the public land near Taos during various times of the year. For information, call New Mexico Game and Fish at (888) 248-6866. Be aware that there may be hunters in the area and wear brightly colored clothing and attach something colorful to your dog's collar as well.

RANCHER ERMINIO MARTINEZ WITH RIVERS & BIRDS HIKING CLUB

FIRE RESTRICTIONS

In times of drought, the Carson National Forest and the Bureau of Land Management may impose restrictions on fires on public lands. There are several stages of restrictions, from minor to a total ban on fires. Once in a great while, public lands may actually be closed to public use, due to extremely high risk of fire. During the summer months, you can call the CNF and BLM or check their websites for more information on current restrictions.

LEAVE NO TRACE

The hikes in this guidebook are on public land that provide natural beauty for those who visit them. Please help preserve this beauty for future generations by packing your trash out, staying on the trail, and leaving the trails as you found them.

WILDERNESS

> *"A wilderness, in contrast with those areas where man and his own works dominate the landscape, is hereby recognized as an area where the earth and its community of life are untrammeled by man, where man himself is a visitor who does not remain."*
>
> — THE WILDERNESS ACT, SIGNED 1964

Some of the hikes in this book are located in wilderness areas, including Latir Peak, Wheeler, Pecos, and the Columbine Hondo Wilderness Area. Wilderness designation prohibits the use of any mechanized devices and ensures that hikers will encounter more undeveloped areas and opportunities for solitude. An effort is made to maintain the wild character of these areas, so you will find fewer formal bridges across creeks and other man-made improvements.

The original Wilderness Act was signed Sept. 3, 1964 and protected 9 million acres in 13 states, including Wheeler Peak and Pecos. The 50th anniversary of the Wilderness Act was celebrated in 2014.

Life Zones

The hikes in this book are found at altitudes ranging from 6,000 to 13,000 feet. You may find yourself in several different climate or life zones during one hike.

THE PRIMARY LIFE ZONES FOUND NEAR TAOS INCLUDE:

Desert/Grassland/Woodlands Zone: Under 7,000 feet

DESERT/GRASSLANDS

This is the combined zone that includes the desert, and as you move higher, the grass and woodland zone. It is often rocky and covered in low-growing shrubs and grasses. This area gets 10-20 inches of rainfall per year and does experience snow. Animals that live here include the jackrabbit, coyote, pronghorn, and mountain lion. During the winter, bald eagles are seen in the Rio Grande Gorge, and many other birds use the gorge as a migratory route. Rattlesnakes live here. Near the Rio Grande, there is a herd of bighorn sheep that began with a group that was relocated from the Wheeler Peak Wilderness. Moving higher in the zone, there are piñon and juniper trees, along with sage and cactus.

Transition (Mountain) Zone: 7,000 to 8,500 feet

VIEW FROM TRANSITION MOUNTAIN ZONE

Beginning at 7,000 feet, ponderosa pine begin to dominate the landscape. These trees can grow up to 150 feet tall and can live 500 years. In this zone, it is wetter and colder than the lower zones. Animals that live here include wild turkey, mule deer and many birds such as the Steller's jay and northern flicker.

Coniferous Forest Zone: 8,500 to 9,500 feet

This zone often has mountain streams that support trees and wildlife. Willows, oaks, aspens, and many wildflowers are found here. Beavers, wild turkey, hummingbirds, American dippers and belted kingfishers are among the animals that live near streams. Douglas fir trees grow tall in this zone, along with aspens.

Black bear, elk, deer and red fox are among the animals that live in the tree-filled areas. Blue grouse are large pheasant-like birds that nest on the ground in groups. If you disturb them, they fly up and away with a startling display of wings and squawking. Open mountain meadows are also found in this zone.

Subalpine: 9,500 to 11,500 feet

Spruce and fir trees grow in this zone that gets 30-60 inches of precipitation per year, including lots of snow. The Engelmann spruce can grow 100 feet tall and has bluish-green needles and pine cones. Elk, mule deer, and bighorn sheep are found in this zone, along with the snowshoe hare, Clark's nutcracker, and many squirrels, chipmunks and woodpeckers.

Alpine: above 11,500 feet

The alpine zone is above tree line and is the most exposed to wind and weather. Small wildflowers and other plants grow close to the ground here. Rocky Mountain bighorn sheep and the golden eagle are among the animals in this zone.

(Primary source for this habitat section is *Life Zones and Habitats of New Mexico*, published by New Mexico Game and Fish.)

CONIFEROUS FOREST ZONE

SUBALPINE ZONE

ALPINE ZONE

Northwest:

WILD RIVERS
& CEBOLLA MESA

Northwest

This section includes the Wild Rivers area and others near the Rio Grande. All of these hikes are best in the spring, fall, or winter or on cool days in the summer. In addition to views of the river, you may see petroglyphs – ancient rock carvings – as well as bighorn sheep or other wildlife.

Rio Grande del Norte National Monument covers most of this area. The new national monument designation means that the area is closed to invasive uses like oil and gas exploration and mining. Traditional uses such as gathering of pine nuts and firewood are specifically allowed, as are hiking, boating, and other recreational activities. The designation means that the natural and cultural resources of the 242,500-acre area will be protected forever, thanks to a presidential proclamation, signed in March 2013.

RED RIVER AND RIO GRANDE CONFLUENCE

For more information: Stop by the BLM Taos Field office at 226 Cruz Alta Road, call (575) 758-8851, or visit http://www.blm.gov/nm/riograndedelnorte.

WILD RIVERS

The Wild Rivers Recreation Area is open all year for hiking and has access to the Rio Grande and Red River. The area is located north of Questa and many of the hikes begin at approximately 7,500 feet and descend to the rivers.

The Wild Rivers Area is part of the Rio Grande Gorge Recreation Area, managed by the Bureau of Land Management (BLM). Wild Rivers includes 22 miles of trails along with five campgrounds and primitive campsites near the rivers. Mountain biking is allowed on some of the trails.

Overlooks: There are two wheelchair accessible overlooks available – one near the entry of the area – the Sheep Crossing Overlook and one at the southern tip of the Backcountry Byway at La Junta campground.

Wild Rivers Visitor Center: To reach the visitor center, go left where the Wild Rivers Backcountry Byway splits. Hours vary by season. In the outside courtyard, there are maps and topographic landforms, as well as comments from visitors on recent wildlife sightings, and bathroom facilities. There is a $3 fee for day use, which can be paid here or at the entry pay station or the trailheads. Maps are available at the visitor center and most of the trailheads, and are very useful for getting oriented.

1. LITTLE ARSENIC SPRINGS

LITTLE ARSENIC SPRING

LENGTH: Just under 2-miles roundtrip

DIFFICULTY: Moderate

ELEVATION: Begins at about 7,500 feet and descends 760 feet to the Rio Grande

HIGHLIGHTS: Views of the Rio Grande, spring crossing

DIRECTIONS: From the Plaza go north about 27 miles on Paseo del Pueblo (which becomes NM 522), passing through Questa. To find Wild Rivers, continue on 2 miles north of Questa. Turn left at NM 378 to Cerro. Follow this road 3.5 miles to the entrance of the Wild Rivers area. Go another 8 miles and turn right at the split to reach the Little Arsenic trailhead.

The Rio Grande is accessible from a series of trailheads located on the western branch of the Wild Rivers Back Country Byway Road. Like many of the trails, the Little Arsenic Springs hike begins at a campground that includes an outhouse facility.

The moderately steep trail follows a series of switchbacks down the side of the gorge, descending about 760 feet. The path passes through scattered piñon and juniper trees where a variety of hawks and other birds may be seen. Volcanic rocks line the descending path, which leads to a flat section just before the river. At this point, the trail joins several others. You can go left on La Junta trail to reach the confluence of the Red River and the Rio Grande. To reach the Little Arsenic Springs, go right less than a half mile. You'll notice the spring crossing the trail at several points. At one of the spring crossings, there is a primitive campsite with a table, shelter, and outhouse that makes a good place to stop for lunch. The trail is about a mile one way.

The Rio Grande here is green, fast and powerful. The river is lined with black basalt rocks created by the cooling of lava flows during the time of volcanic activity now long past.

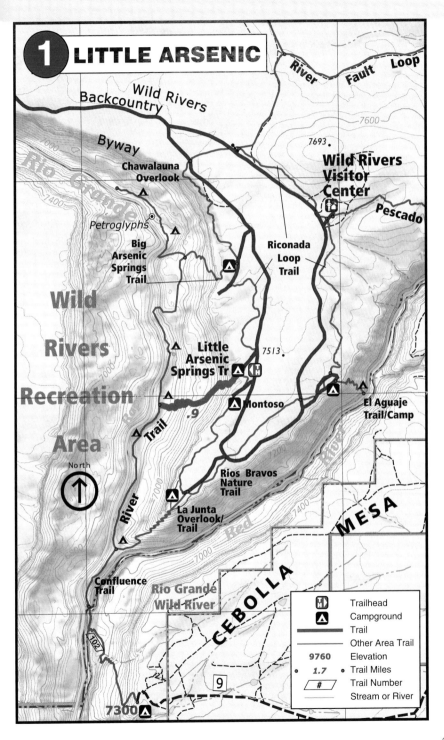

1 LITTLE ARSENIC

River Fault Loop

Wild Rivers
Backcountry
Byway

7693.

Wild Rivers
Visitor
Center

Pescado

Chawalauna
Overlook

Rio Grande

7600

7400

Petroglyphs

Big
Arsenic
Springs
Trail

Riconada
Loop
Trail

Wild

Rivers

Recreation

Area

Little
Arsenic
Springs Tr

7513.

Montoso

El Aguaje
Trail/Camp

.9

Trail

North

↑

River

Rios Bravos
Nature
Trail

La Junta
Overlook/
Trail

River

7400

MESA

7000

Red

7000

Confluence
Trail

Rio Grande
Wild River

CEBOLLA

102

| | Trailhead |
| Campground |
| Trail |
	Other Area Trail
9760	Elevation
1.7	Trail Miles
#	Trail Number
	Stream or River

9

7300

25

2. BIG ARSENIC SPRINGS

BIG ARSENIC SPRINGS

LENGTH: Just under 2-miles roundtrip to river; an additional .5-mile to the petroglyphs

DIFFICULTY: Moderate

ELEVATION: Begins at about 7,500 feet and descends 700 feet to the Rio Grande

HIGHLIGHTS: Views of the Rio Grande, petroglyphs

DIRECTIONS: From the Taos Plaza, head north on Paseo del Pueblo (which becomes NM 522) for about 27 miles, passing through Questa. To find Wild Rivers, continue on 2 miles north of Questa. Turn left at NM 378 to Cerro. Follow this road 3.5 miles to the entrance of the Wild Rivers area. Go another 8 miles and turn right at the split to reach the Big Arsenic trailhead. There are outhouse facilities here and at the camping area at the bottom of the gorge.

The trail begins at an elevation of approximately 7,500 feet. It drops along a series of switchbacks lined with rock walls. Signs along the way describe the towering piñon pines, along with other vegetation and geology. The hike passes through meadows surrounded by basalt outcroppings, with the rocky cliffs of the gorge rim above. Near the river, this path connects to the Little Arsenic and La Junta trails.

After just under a mile of hiking and a descent of about 700 feet, you arrive at Big Arsenic Spring as it flows into the Rio Grande. This cool water spring contains traces of natural occurring arsenic, as do others in the area. Although not considered to be dangerous in small quantities, drinking from this and other springs is not recommended.

Just beyond the Big Arsenic, there are camping shelters and picnic tables. This is a great place to stop for lunch and listen to the river just below. Also here are petroglyphs – pictures carved in stone by the people passing through the gorge in the past.

Merrill Dicks, archeologist with the Bureau of Land Management (BLM), says that this area has been used by Native American tribes, shepherds and home-steaders. He explains that in locations that lend themselves to camping, petroglyphs are often found nearby. Depictions of animals and humans found here may have been carved by Pueblo Indians nearly 1,000 years ago. Other symbols associated with this period are snakes, rain, water, and deities governing fertility for crops. Some of the petroglyphs of crosses and other symbols may have been left in the early historic period, around 1600, by Spanish explorers. Ancestors of the Utes, along with Comanche, Apache and Kiowa Indians, are known to have passed through this area and told their stories through rock carvings as well.

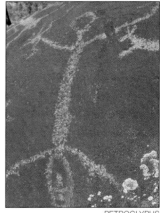
PETROGLYPHS

The presence of the petroglyphs is a dramatic reminder of all the human history that has occurred in the Rio Grande Gorge. Dicks explains that the BLM works to find the right balance between allowing visitors to enjoy the experience of seeing the petroglyphs and at the same time protecting and preserving these and other artifacts for the future. He says it is fine to photograph the carvings, but not to climb on the rocks, touch the figures, or disturb the vegetation. He says that the oil from human hands can cause deterioration of the carvings, as can rubbing over them with paper and pencil.

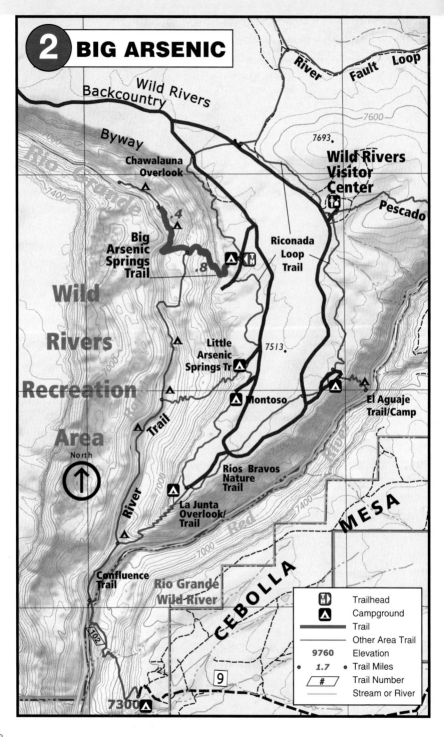

2 BIG ARSENIC

River Fault Loop

Wild Rivers Backcountry Byway

7600

7693.

Rio Grande

7400

Chawalauna Overlook

Wild Rivers Visitor Center

Pescado

4

Big Arsenic Springs Trail

.8

Riconada Loop Trail

Wild

7000

Rivers

Little Arsenic Springs Tr

7513.

Recreation

Montoso

El Aguaje Trail/Camp

Area

North

Rios Bravos Nature Trail

7700

River

River

La Junta Overlook/ Trail

7400

MESA

7000

Red

Confluence Trail

Rio Grande Wild River

CEBOLLA

102

9

7300

🚻	Trailhead
🔺	Campground
▬▬	Trail
──	Other Area Trail
9760	Elevation
• 1.7 •	Trail Miles
#	Trail Number
──	Stream or River

3. LAS VISTAS DE QUESTA

AARON RAEL MEMORIAL

Another way to reach the Wild Rivers Area is to begin a hike at the Punto del Coyote/Las Vistas de Questa Trail. This trailhead is located closer to Questa – look for the signs just north of town. From the parking area, walk west along a path between fields. The trail climbs through pine and scrub oak trees, becoming moderately steep. A lower overlook offers views back into Questa and the Columbine Hondo Wilderness to the east. Continue to climb and follow the signs to the higher overlook, where there is a bench dedicated to Aaron Rael, the late Questa native and assistant manager of the Wild Rivers area. One of Aaron's last projects was to design the bench.

You can descend the trail and return the way you came or follow a loop to the north. To reach the Wild Rivers Area, continue west at the junction sign to the trailhead located on the Back Country Byway. This trail was completed in 2010, a cooperative effort of the BLM, the Village of Questa, Rocky Mountain Youth Corp, and Chevron.

LENGTH: 3-miles roundtrip to Punto del Coyote overlook and 14-miles roundtrip to Wild Rivers

DIFFICULTY: Moderate

ELEVATION: Begins at 7,600 feet and ascends to 8,200 feet at Punto del Coyote overlook

HIGHLIGHTS: Views into Questa and of the Sangre de Cristos to the east

DIRECTIONS: From the Plaza and Paseo del Pueblo, go north about 26 miles on Paseo (which becomes NM 522), passing through Questa. To reach Las Vistas de Questa trailhead, look for the sign before mile marker 22, just north of town. Turn left and follow a dirt road another mile to the trailhead. To find Wild Rivers, go another mile farther on NM 522 and turn left at NM 378 to Cerro. Follow this road 3.5 miles to the entrance of the Wild Rivers area. Another 8.5 miles will bring you to the visitor center.

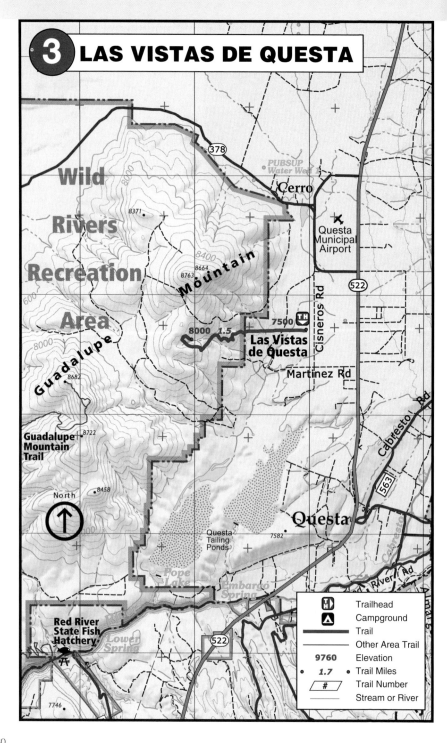

3 LAS VISTAS DE QUESTA

378

PUBSUP
Water Well

Cerro

8371

Wild

Rivers

Questa
Municipal
Airport

8400

522

Recreation

8664
8763

Mountain

7500

8000 1.5

Las Vistas
de Questa

Area

Cisneros Rd

8000

Guadalupe

Martinez Rd

8682

Cabresto Rd

Guadalupe
Mountain
Trail

8722

563

North

8458

Questa

Questa
Tailing
Ponds

7582

River Rd

Pope
Lake

Embargo
Spring

Cabresto

Red River
State Fish
Hatchery

Lower
Spring

522

Almita

7746

	Trailhead
	Campground
	Trail
	Other Area Trail
9760	Elevation
1.7	Trail Miles
#	Trail Number
	Stream or River

4. CEBOLLA MESA (CNF #102)

BASALT BOULDERS

LENGTH: 2.6-miles roundtrip

DIFFICULTY: Moderate

ELEVATION: Begins at 7,300 feet and drops 1,000 feet

HIGHLIGHTS: Bird sightings near the river; black basalt rocks

DIRECTIONS: From the Plaza and Paseo del Pueblo, drive north 19 miles on Paseo del Pueblo Norte/NM 522. Turn left on Forest Road 9, just after mile marker 15. Continue on the dirt road an additional 3.3 miles to the trailhead. The road is signed "not suitable for passenger vehicles." If the road is dry, it is generally passable for most vehicles, although there are a few large ruts. If it is wet, it is more challenging. There is an outhouse, along with campsites and picnic tables at the trailhead.

Cebolla Mesa is just to the south of Wild Rivers; it is managed by the Carson National Forest. It is reached by driving north on NM 522 from Taos 19 miles and turning left (west) on Forest Road 9. Similar to Wild Rivers, the Cebolla Mesa trail leads down to the Rio Grande. Cebolla Mesa is the only trail in the Carson National Forest (CNF) that accesses the Rio Grande. Most of the other trails in the area are managed by the Bureau of Land Management (BLM). In the past, there was a log bridge that crossed the Red River, connecting the Cebolla Mesa trail with the BLM Wild Rivers area to the north. Several years ago, the bridge broke in half and it has not been replaced. The BLM and Carson National Forest are working together to explore ways to replace the bridge.

The Cebolla (Wild Onion) Mesa trail begins on the rim of the gorge at 7,300 feet. The trail follows some moderately steep switchbacks down from the rocky cliff edge. It then enters a flatter shelf and crosses some small meadows, marked by rock formations and areas of piñon and juniper. The final stretch contains longer switchbacks, which bring you down to the big basalt boulders that line the Rio Grande. The descent covers about 1.3 miles and drops almost 1,000 feet.

As you descend into the gorge, you'll hear the rushing sound of the Rio Grande growing louder. The black basalt rocks along the river hold the sun and warm the area near the riverbank, creating nice spots for resting or picnicking. The trail ends near the confluence of the Red River and the Rio Grande.

In 1968, Congress protected eight rivers with the Wild and Scenic designation. This section of the Rio Grande was among the original rivers included in this river system, as was the lower 4 miles of the Red River. To preserve water quality and historic beauty and uses, all rivers in the Wild and Scenic system are to remain free flowing. In New Mexico, 124 miles of river have this protection, including 68 miles of the Rio Grande from the Colorado border south.

Wildlife: On this hike, I have seen the American dipper bird perching on the rocks in the Red River and bobbing its head under the water. Francisco Cortez, wildlife program manager for the Carson National Forest, says that the dipper bird puts its head under water to look for insect larvae just below the surface.

Cortez says that fall and winter are good times to see wildlife along the Rio Grande. As ponds and lakes begin to freeze, migrating waterfowl are attracted to the flowing river. Bald eagles may be seen flying through the gorge in search of fish or carrion.

Deer, elk, and bighorn sheep are also drawn to the water and may be visible near the river. Cortez says that with these big game animals come predators, such as mountain lions and coyotes. Although hikers may see scat or other signs, it is quite rare to actually see these predators.

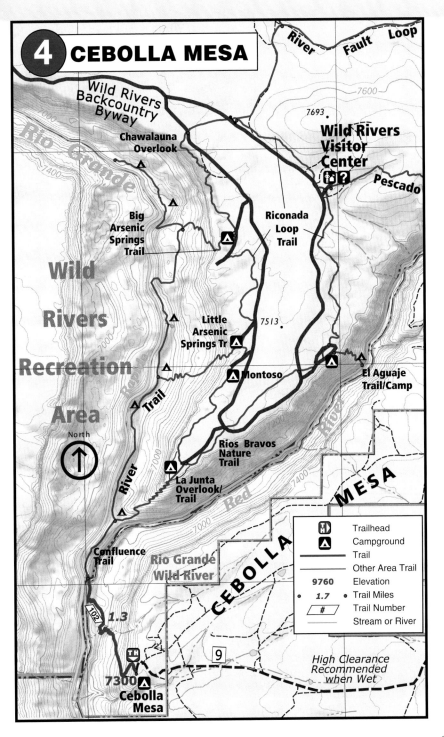

4 CEBOLLA MESA

River Fault Loop

Wild Rivers Backcountry Byway

7600

7693

Chawalauna Overlook

Wild Rivers Visitor Center

Rio Grande

7400

Pescado

Big Arsenic Springs Trail

Riconada Loop Trail

Wild

Rivers

7513

Little Arsenic Springs Tr

Recreation

Montoso

El Aguaje Trail/Camp

Area

North

Rapa Trail

River

Red River

Rios Bravos Nature Trail

7000

La Junta Overlook/ Trail

7400

MESA

Confluence Trail

Rio Grande Wild River

7000

CEBOLLA

102 1.3

9

High Clearance Recommended when Wet

7300 Cebolla Mesa

	Trailhead
	Campground
	Trail
	Other Area Trail
9760	Elevation
1.7	Trail Miles
#	Trail Number
	Stream or River

Northeast:

COLUMBINE HONDO, WHEELER & LATIR PEAK

Northeast

Along the Ski Valley Road (NM 150), there are four trails in the Carson National Forest that lead to Lobo Ridge and Lobo Peak. The four trails are Yerba, Manzanita, Italianos, and Gavilan. Lobo Ridge connects the trails and varies in altitude at different points.

These are great hikes in the summer with cool aspen groves and creek crossings. From the ski area itself, you can hike to Long Canyon, or Gold Hill among other destinations. Another set of trails may be accessed from north of Questa, including Columbine Canyon. All of these trails are part of the Columbine Hondo Wilderness Area.

The area encompasses 46,000 acres of the Sangre de Christo Mountains that includes the trails accessed from the Ski Valley Road and the Taos ski area.

The wilderness designation was made permanent in 2015. The protection of this area preserves the headwaters of the Upper Rio Grande – the Red River and the Rio Hondo – ensuring clean water for downstream agricultural communities. The Taos Pueblo has been a leader in the effort to ensure permanent wilderness designation, believing that wilderness is sacred and that humans have a responsibility to protect the land.

Since 1924, when the Gila Wilderness was recognized as the first wilderness in the United States, there has been an understanding of the crucial role that wild lands play in the health of the earth and the well-being of people. Aldo Leopold worked to bring about the action that created the Gila, even before there was wilderness legislation. Leopold was the first supervisor of the Carson National Forest in 1912 and is often referred to as the father of wilderness. He is credited with writing an essay that sparked the environmental movement. The cabin where he wrote the famous essay is still standing and can be seen behind the Ranger Station at Tres Piedras.

Also from the ski valley, you can reach Williams Lake and Wheeler Peak, which are part of the Wheeler Wilderness. Wheeler Peak is the highest mountain in New Mexico at 13,161 feet.

Near Questa, Cabresto Lake is the jumping-off point for access to the Latir Peak Wilderness. The hike from Cabresto Lake to Heart Lake is included in this section.

South Columbine Hondo: Taos Ski Valley Road Access

5. YERBA CANYON (CNF #61)

BUTTERFLY ON CONE FLOWER

Yerba Canyon Trail is the closest hike to town on the Ski Valley Road. Head up NM 150 toward Taos Ski Valley. The trailhead is located just after mile marker 10. The trail follows a creek and if you hike one to two hours up the trail, you will cross the creek as many as 16 times.

The hike begins in a canyon with rock formations and passes through a wooded area with aspens and evergreens. You may see wildlife, including the large pheasant-like birds known as blue grouse along with their chicks. Among the unusual features to look for on this trail are two wooden crosses nailed to a tree at creek crossing #4.

If you continue up the trail after the 16th creek crossing, you will begin a climb up away from the creek. You can hike on another hour and a half or more to reach the ridge and an additional half-hour to reach Lobo Peak. It is 3.9 miles to the ridge and 4.3 miles to Lobo Peak.

LENGTH: To Lobo Ridge, 7.8-miles roundtrip. To Lobo Peak, 8.6-miles roundtrip

DIFFICULTY: Moderate along creek, more difficult to ridge and Lobo Peak

ELEVATION: Begins at 8,200 feet. Lobo Ridge is 11,800 feet and Lobo Peak at 12,115 feet.

HIGHLIGHTS: Creek crossings, possible bird sightings including blue grouse

DIRECTIONS: From Taos Plaza, take Paseo del Pueblo Norte (US 64) 4 miles to the intersection of US 64, NM 522 and the Ski Valley Road. Turn right at the Ski Valley Road (NM 150). Take this road through Arroyo Seco; bear left at the old school; look for the sign that says Ski Valley with an arrow pointing left. Continue up to just past mile marker 10. There is parking off to the right side; the trail is on the left.

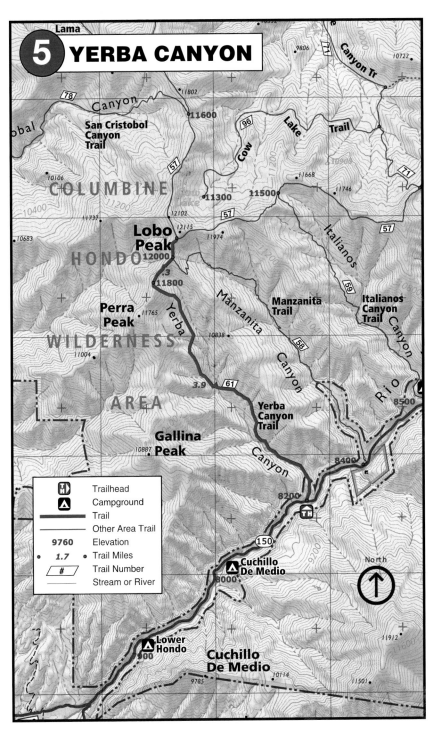

5 YERBA CANYON

Lama

San Cristobol Canyon Trail

Canyon Tr

Canyon

Lake Trail

Cow

COLUMBINE

Lobo Peak

HONDO 12000

Perra Peak

WILDERNESS

Italianos

Manzanita Trail

Italianos Canyon Trail

Manzanita

AREA

Yerba

Canyon

Yerba Canyon Trail

Gallina Peak

Canyon

Rio

Legend

🏠	Trailhead
⛺	Campground
▬	Trail
—	Other Area Trail
9760	Elevation
• *1.7* •	Trail Miles
⬡ #	Trail Number
~~	Stream or River

Cuchillo De Medio

Lower Hondo

Cuchillo De Medio

North ↑

6. MANZANITA CANYON TRAIL (CNF #58)

MANZANITA CANYON

LENGTH: To Lobo Ridge 8.4-miles roundtrip; to Lobo Peak 8.6-miles roundtrip

DIFFICULTY: Moderate at the beginning, becoming more challenging to the ridge and peak

ELEVATION: Begins at 8,400 feet; Lobo Ridge 12,000 feet and Lobo Peak 12,115 feet.

HIGHLIGHTS: Fewer creek crossings in lower sections; one of the quickest ways to Lobo Peak

DIRECTIONS: From Taos Plaza, go north on Paseo del Pueblo (US 64) 4 miles. Turn right at the Ski Valley Road (NM 150). Take this road through Arroyo Seco; bear left at the old school. Continue up to mile marker 11. There is parking on the left side of the road, where the trail begins.

Manzanita Canyon Trail starts in a wood of aspen and evergreen. There is one creek crossing early on. Unlike the nearby trails Yerba and Italianos, this one does not have numerous creek crossings in the lower section, making it an easier alternative during the snowy winter months or during times of high run-off.

After about 30 minutes of steady climbing, you will see 'the park,' an open area off to the right under a rock cliff. This area makes a great destination for a short hike. After this point, the trail continues alongside the creek.

On the higher sections, the path begins to cross the creek with more frequency. There are nine creek crossings in the next 30 minutes to hour of hiking. After the ninth crossing, you begin to climb out of the creek area on the right side to a section that includes some steep areas interspersed with flatter meadows. From the trailhead, it is 4.2 miles to the ridge, with Lobo Peak just beyond.

According to Craig Saum with the Carson National Forest, "Manzanita is the quickest route to the top of Lobo Peak, and the views up there always make it worth the effort. Manzanita Trail (#58) meets Yerba Trail (#61), and from there it is a short steep segment to the top of Lobo Peak. The CNF trail crew helped with maintenance efforts recently, including some badly needed brush removal and signage re-installation in the higher sections that will definitely result in a better hiking experience as the route is now more established and easier to follow."

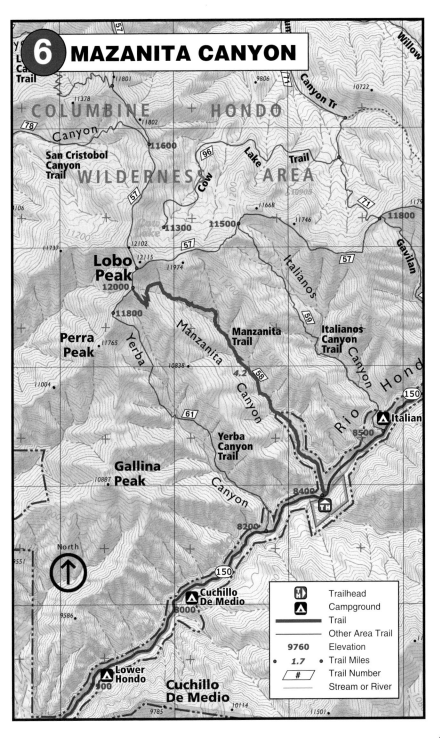

6 MAZANITA CANYON

COLUMBINE + HONDO

78 Canyon

San Cristobol
Canyon
Trail

WILDERNESS AREA

Lobo
Peak
12000

Perra
Peak

Manzanita
Trail

Italianos
Canyon
Trail

Yerba

Manzanita

4.2

Yerba
Canyon
Trail

Gallina
Peak

Canyon

Italian

8500

8400

8200

North

150

Cuchillo
De Medio

Lower
Hondo

Cuchillo
De Medio

	Trailhead
	Campground
——	Trail
——	Other Area Trail
9760	Elevation
• 1.7 •	Trail Miles
#	Trail Number
——	Stream or River

7. ITALIANOS CANYON (CNF #59)

CALYPSO LADY SLIPPER ORCHID

LENGTH: To Lobo Ridge and back 7.4-miles; to Lobo Peak 10-miles

DIFFICULTY: Moderate in the canyon; difficult to the ridge and peak

ELEVATION: Begins at 8,600 feet; Lobo Ridge 11,500 feet and Lobo Peak 12,115 feet.

HIGHLIGHTS: Creek crossings, aspen groves, rock formations

DIRECTIONS: From Taos Plaza, go north on Paseo del Pueblo (US 64) 4 miles. Turn right at the Ski Valley Road (NM 150). Take this road through Arroyo Seco; bear left at the old school. Continue up to mile marker 12. There is parking on both sides of the road and up a short four-wheel drive entry.

Italianos is a beautiful hike and it follows a creek for the first hour or more. The rock ledges of the canyon and in the creek distinguish this hike from some of the others accessed from the Ski Valley Road.

The lower creek section is usually shady, breezy, and cool. The trail crosses the creek 11 times on logs and stones. Doing all the creek crossings is an accomplishment in itself. During the spring and early summer run-off, the creek can be high. The rocks and logs that allow for creek crossing can be slippery – so proceed cautiously and consider carrying a hiking pole or stick to help with balance on the crossings. After the eighth crossing, several small side springs flow into the creek and you will often see many purple, white, and yellow butterflies here. After crossing the springs, you will reach the first large leafy-green aspen grove. With the trees swaying overhead in the breeze, the grove is a pleasant place to stop and rest.

In the summer, this section of the trail has a variety of wild flowers including the red columbine, wild geranium, chiming bells, rocky mountain clematis, and the rare and exotic calypso lady slipper orchid. This flower "depends on a symbiotic relationship with a soil-borne fungus. You should consider yourself very lucky if you see this spectacular flower," according to the *Rocky Mountain Wildflowers Pocket Guide* by David Dahms.

After the last crossing, the trail leaves the creek and begins to climb up a series of switchbacks. The climb is steep in sections, leveling out as you approach the first small meadow. This meadow can be reached between one hour and a quarter and two hours into the hike, if you are hiking briskly. You can proceed to the second, larger meadow and then the ridge. It is about 3.7 miles total to Lobo Ridge that connects the trails on the Ski Valley Road and another 1.3 miles to Lobo Peak. The ridge can be reached in two to three hours and the return trip will be somewhat shorter. I find that for every hour going up, it usually takes about 50 minutes to come down. As you go higher, be aware of the chance of an afternoon thunderstorm. Italianos is a popular trail, especially on the weekends in the summer.

History: The trail is named after an Italian, Carlo Prandi, according to local descendants of the Prandi family, including Paul Martinez of Paul's Men Shop. Carlo was born in 1836 in Piedmonte, Italy and came to New Mexico at the age of 16. He traveled with his uncle, a Catholic priest, who was killed by Native Americans in Socorro. Carlo made his way to the archdiocese in Santa Fe, where he became a chef for Bishop Lamy. Carlo later came to Taos and bought land in Valdez to establish a flour mill. He also owned land in the canyon, now known as Italianos Canyon. Cows and horses were pastured there. Many descendants of Carlo Prandi and the French woman he married live in Valdez and Arroyo Hondo today.

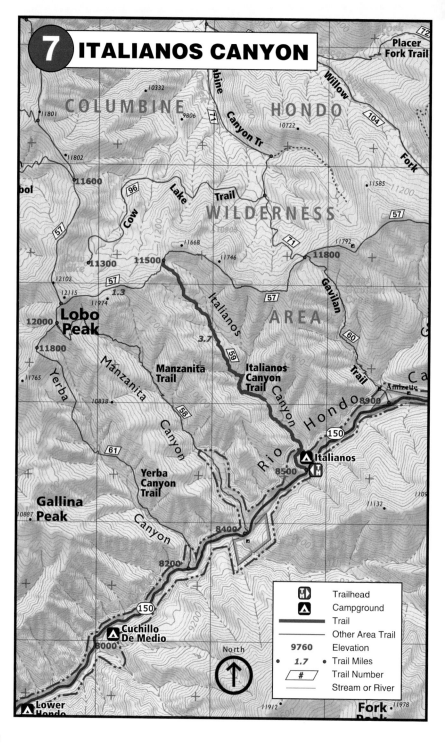

8. GAVILAN (HAWK) CNF #60

GAVILAN FALLS

LENGTH: 5-miles roundtrip to Lobo Ridge

DIFFICULTY: Moderate at the beginning, becoming steeper after the creek crossing

ELEVATION: Begins at 9,000 feet; Lobo Ridge 11,800 feet.

HIGHLIGHTS: Shortest, steepest way to Lobo Ridge, wildflowers, and Gavilan Falls

DIRECTIONS: From Taos Plaza, go north on Paseo del Pueblo Norte (US 64) 4 miles. Turn right at the Ski Valley Road (NM 150). Take this road through Arroyo Seco; bear left at the old school. Continue up to mile marker 13. There is parking on both sides of the road.

The hike is moderately steep at the beginning, and there is one crossing of West Gavilan Creek, about 20 minutes into the hike. As you leave the creek, the trail becomes more challenging in places. You can look down to the left of the trail into the ravine, as the trail climbs away from the creek. There are flatter areas interspersed with the more vertical sections, as you enter the forest. Wildflowers bloom later here due to the high elevation, and you may see the scarlet gilia fairy trumpet, wild geraniums, asters, and fireweed, along with wild raspberries. Blue grouse, a large pheasant-like bird, is sometimes seen on this trail, along with mule deer.

Gavilan Falls: Before the most challenging part of the hike, at about 40 minutes, you will see a sign to the left marked Gavilan Falls ¼ mile. A short walk down this trail brings you to a view of a waterfall.

The first time I visited the waterfall, I wanted to explore the way to get to the bottom of the falls. After finding myself on the ledge, I tried to make my way down a very steep incline. Part of the hillside gave way, and I went sliding and tumbling down about 50 feet and landed at the edge of the creek. After reaching the bottom of the hill, bloody and dirty, but with no broken bones, I managed to take a picture of the falls, before I clawed my way back up the hill. If I had not had two poles with me, I would have had a very difficult time getting out of the ravine. A round trip to the falls can be done in about an hour and a quarter – not including the slide into the creek.

The first meadow: Continuing on the main trail, you can expect to arrive at the first meadow anytime after an hour and a quarter from the trailhead. This is a long meadow, followed by two shorter ones, from which you can see the Taos Ski Valley. It is a great place to end your hike or rest before the final ascent.

Lobo Ridge: You can reach the ridge by hiking 1-1/2 hours to 2 hours total. From the trailhead to the ridge, the hike is 2.5 miles – shorter than the Italianos hike, which is 3.7 miles. If you go up to the right toward Gold Hill just a little ways, you will have spectacular views to the north into San Cristobal. Gold Hill (12,711 ft) is 4.5 miles to the east. Lobo Peak (12,115 ft) is 3.5 miles to the west.

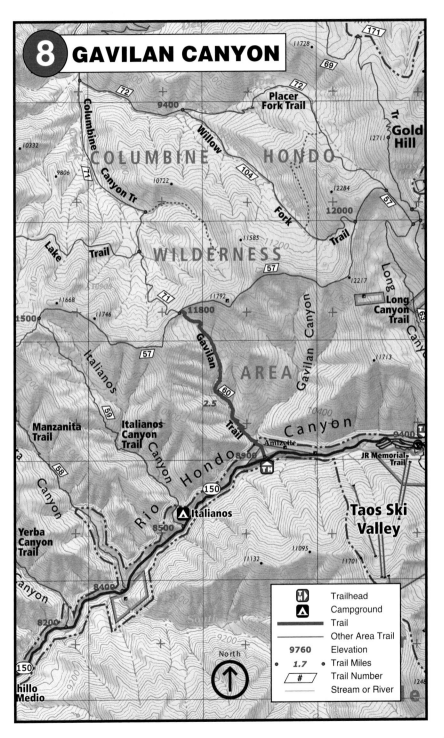

8 GAVILAN CANYON

45

9. LONG CANYON TO GOLD HILL (CNF #63 AND #64)

The hike begins on a moderately steep incline up Bull-of-the-Woods trail. The path follows the East Fork of the Rio Hondo through the spruce and fir trees, making it cool and comfortable. In the summer, there are columbine and wild geranium flowers, along with wild strawberries and raspberries. Continue along Bull-of-the-Woods for just under a mile. Turn left at the sign that says *Long Canyon #63*. Walk along the creek; there are a series of meadows to the left of the trail. The meadows are a great place to end a shorter hike or to rest before beginning the climb to Gold Hill.

VIEW RETURNING FROM GOLD HILL SUMMIT

LENGTH: 9-miles roundtrip

DIFFICULTY: Moderate along Bull-of-the-Woods and Long Canyon; more difficult to Gold Hill

ELEVATION: Begins at 9,400 feet and climbs to the Gold Hill summit at over 12,700 feet.

HIGHLIGHTS: Wildflowers in summer along two creeks, fantastic views from Gold Hill

DIRECTIONS: From Taos Plaza, go north on Paseo del Pueblo (US 64) approximately 4 miles. Turn right at the Ski Valley Road (NM 150). Take this road through Arroyo Seco and bear left at the old school. Continue up to Taos Ski Valley, stay left and drive into the upper parking lots. Look for the trailhead on the left (northeast) side of the lot, near the Twining Campground. It is a total of 20 miles from the center of town and 10 miles from the Arroyo Seco post office. There is a bathroom building here. Beginning in 2014, this area has been under construction to accommodate changes at Taos Ski Valley. Access to trailheads is usually maintained, but minor changes to the area can be expected.

After leaving Long Canyon, turn right at the fork in the trail. The trail traverses a steep hillside covered by tall trees and boulders perched on the edge. Emerging into a large meadow, the path meets the Gold Hill Trail. An additional climb of 45 minutes to an hour through grassy and rocky terrain brings you to the summit. The ascent takes about three hours of steady walking.

It is often windy at the top; a rock shelter facing west provides some protection. From the summit you can look down on to the Taos Ski Valley and across to Kachina Peak, or down into the Columbine Hondo area on the Questa side. The hike is 9 miles long and takes about 5 hours round trip.

According to Francisco Cortez, wildlife biologist with the Carson National Forest, the riparian areas along the trails lend themselves to wildlife, including elk, deer, bear, migratory birds, and grouse. Animals in the wilderness adapt to human presence by staying away from the trails during the day and returning to the canyon for water during the early morning and evening hours, so it is not common to see wildlife along the creeks. Heading higher onto the ridges and open meadows, it is likely that hikers will encounter small mammals such as marmots, chipmunks, squirrels, and pika. Bigger animals including elk, deer, and bighorn sheep are also seen at higher elevations.

Weather: The ski valley is usually several degrees cooler than town. Even cooler temperatures and windy conditions can be encountered as you move higher. By mid-summer, there is often a pattern of clear mornings followed by afternoon thunderstorms. Cortez reminds hikers to be aware of lightning, especially on exposed mountains tops and ridges.

Many people don't know that there is private land accessed from the Taos Ski Valley. Northside at Taos Ski Valley is a fee-based recreation area. Day and season passes are available for hiking and mountain biking. Many of the Northside trails connect with Carson trails. For more information, call (575) 776-3233.

9 LONG CANYON - GOLD HILL

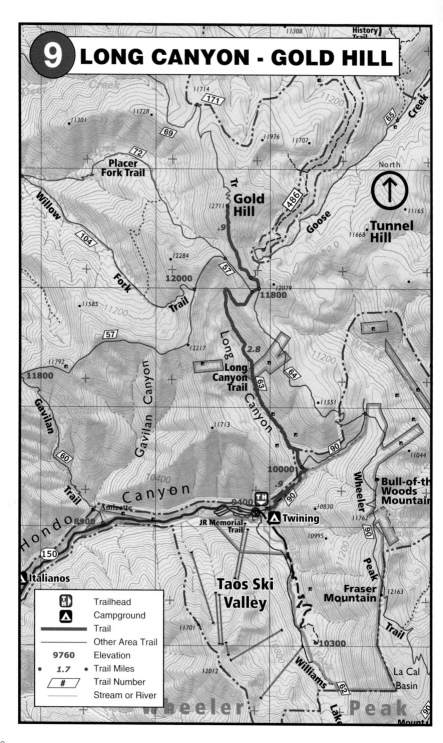

Legend:
- Trailhead
- Campground
- Trail
- Other Area Trail
- 9760 Elevation
- 1.7 Trail Miles
- # Trail Number
- Stream or River

North Columbine Hondo from Questa

10. COLUMBINE CANYON TRAIL (CNF #71)

BLUE COLUMBINE

Beginning at Columbine Campground between Questa and Red River, a network of trails offers access to the woods and meadows leading to Lobo Ridge, Lobo Peak, and Gold Hill. This approach from the north is more moderate in difficulty, but longer in distance than the south approach accessed from the Ski Valley Road. To reach Lobo Ridge that connects these peaks from the Columbine Canyon trail, hikers must cover almost 6 miles, compared with just 2.5 miles to reach the same point on the Gavilan Canyon trail that begins near Taos Ski Valley.

The Columbine Canyon Trail is well traveled in its lower sections, but as you move farther along the path, it is quieter and

LENGTH: 12-miles roundtrip to ridge

DIFFICULTY: Moderate in lower sections, more difficult close to the ridge

ELEVATION: 8,000 feet to 11,800 feet

HIGHLIGHTS: Blue columbine and other wildflowers in summer, hike along Columbine Creek

DIRECTIONS: From Taos Plaza, go north on Paseo del Pueblo, which becomes NM 522, for about 24 miles to Questa. Turn right at State Highway 38. Pass the Questa Ranger Station on the right and the Chevron Mine on the left. Near mile marker 5, turn right at the Columbine Campground entrance, follow the one-way loop to the left and go 0.5 miles to the trailhead, located across the road from the bathroom facilities.

also greener, due to frequent late afternoon showers. Beginning at 8,000 feet, the trail climbs gradually and there are two short steep sections, near the beginning. The creek can be heard below, and soon there is a series of four bridges that cross it. The trail meanders through a woods of aspen and alder, and there is a small meadow that provides a good place to end a shorter hike or to rest before continuing.

Three more informal creek crossings follow, and along the way are the turns for the Deer Creek Trail, Placer Fork, and Willow Fork Trails that lead to Gold Hill. After approximately 1.5 miles of hiking, there is a large meadow that is a popular destination. Beyond this point, the trail becomes steeper and follows a series of switchbacks. The creek drops longer distances, creating waterfalls over moss-covered rocks. In this upper section, ferns grow in the shaded areas near the water. In the summer, wild raspberry and strawberry, red columbine, and blue chiming bells grow in this section.

A third meadow is marked by two large rocks. After this point, the trail becomes steeper and climbs another mile and a half through old growth forest to reach the ridge at 11,800 feet. Here the Columbine Canyon Trail connects with the Gavilan Canyon Trail. There are dramatic views of the Columbine Hondo area spread out below and Latir Peak to the north.

Wildlife: Many small squirrels and chipmunks are visible near the trail and songbirds can be heard. Visitors might also see mule deer, elk, antelope, black bear, mountain lion or bighorn sheep, although those are rarely seen.

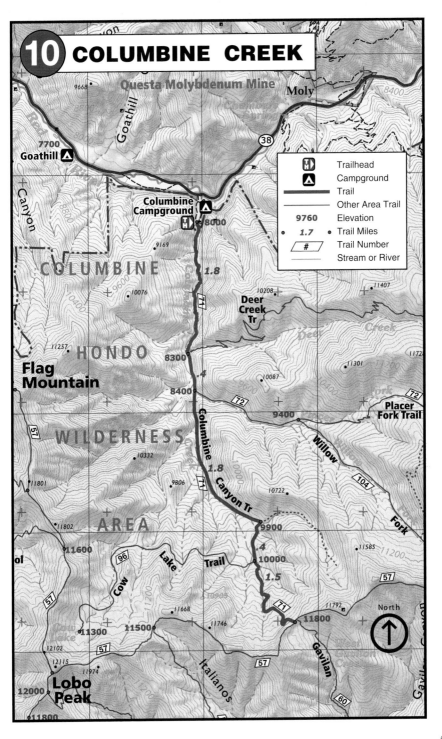

10 COLUMBINE CREEK

Questa Molybdenum Mine
Moly

9668

Goathill
8400
38

7700
Goathill

Canyon

Columbine
Campground
8000

COLUMBINE
1.8

9169

9600
10076

HONDO
8300

Flag
Mountain
11257

WILDERNESS
8400

10332

57

AREA

9806

11801

11802

11600
96

Cow
Lake
Trail

ol

11300
11500

11668
11746

12102

12115
57

11974

Lobo
Peak
12000

11800

10208
Deer
Creek
Tr

11407

Deer   Creek

11301
11172

10087

72
9400

Placer
Fork Trail
72

Willow

104

Fork
57

10722

9900

.4
10000

1.5

71
11792
11800

11585

North

Italianos
57

Gavilan
60

Legend

	Trailhead
	Campground
	Trail
	Other Area Trail
9760	Elevation
1.7	Trail Miles
#	Trail Number
	Stream or River

11. SAN CRISTOBAL CANYON (CNF #78)

If you are looking for a new way to explore the Columbine Hondo area, the San Cristobal Canyon trail offers a quiet, less-traveled option. To reach the trailhead requires driving on some gravel and four-wheel roads, but the pay-off is a cool, shady hike along San Cristobal Creek, usually without many other people on the trail.

From the trailhead, a brief downhill walk leads to the creek. Here the piñon and juniper spread low over the bare, gravelly ground. The path follows San Cristobal Creek and crosses it 15 times, before beginning the climb up toward the ridge. Large old growth ponderosa and Douglas firs dominate the forest. The trail passes

SAN CRISTOBAL CREEK

LENGTH: Just over 9-miles roundtrip to the ridge

DIFFICULTY: Moderate in lower sections, more difficult near the top

ELEVATION: 8,500 feet to 11,600 at the ridge

HIGHLIGHTS: Follows San Cristobal Creek, wildflowers in summer, views from the ridge, shady and cool in summer

DIRECTIONS: From the center of town at Taos Plaza, drive north 4 miles on Paseo del Pueblo to the intersection with the Ski Valley Road. Continue straight onto NM 522 toward Questa. Near mile marker 11, turn right at the San Cristobal sign, County Road B-009. Drive just under a mile along Old Highway 3. Turn left at Camino del Medio. The road turns to gravel here and continues 1.5 miles, past the church, a store, and San Cristobal Headstart to the San Cristobal Academy. There is a pullout where you can park. If you have a high clearance vehicle, you can drive an additional 1.2 miles to the trailhead. This section of the road has some deep ruts and if there has been rain, it can be muddy. Total mileage is approximately 18.5 miles.

through rocky canyon walls and near moss-covered boulders. During the summer, wildflowers bloom along the creek, including scarlet paintbrush, delicate fuchsia fireweed, deep purple monkshood, and maroon dusky penstemon.

The uphill switchbacks take you through an aspen grove that leads to a big meadow, which is a good place to end a shorter hike or to stop for lunch. From this point, the trail follows a dry creek bed up a gradual incline that becomes steeper as it comes closer to the ridge. Recently a group of volunteers working with the Carson National Forest cleared out most of the deadfall on the trail; however, there are still some large trees that block the trail and require some out of direction travel to get around them in the upper reaches.

The trail is hard to follow in places, but cairns (piles of rocks) mark the most difficult sections. After another series of switchbacks, the trail reaches Lobo Ridge at 11,600 feet. Near the top, there are views back into San Cristobal and out to the Taos Plateau. From the ridge, Lobo Peak is visible to the south, and a trail to the north leads to Flag Mountain.

Walking briskly, it can take more than 3 hours to ridge and another 2.5 hours for the return. A hike of this length requires some planning and stamina to complete. Although reaching the Lobo Ridge or one of the nearby mountains can be physically demanding, the reward is peaceful hiking along the trail, which is sometimes moist with rain and surrounded by wildflowers.

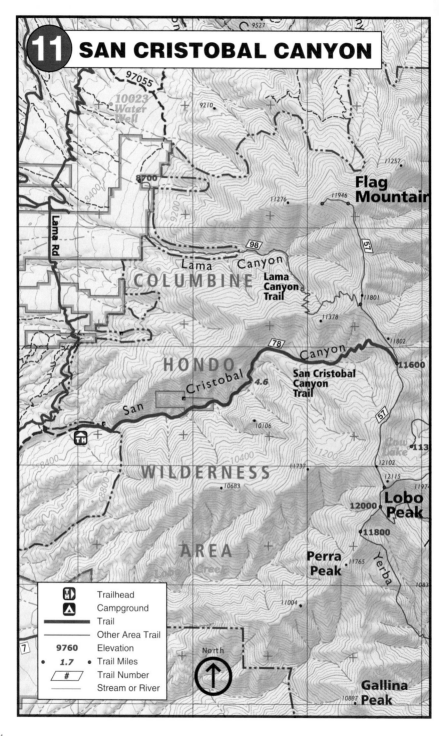

11 SAN CRISTOBAL CANYON

97055

10023
Water
Well

9210

9527

11257

Flag
Mountain

11276   11946

Lama Rd

8700

98

57

Lama   Canyon
COLUMBINE   Lama
Canyon
Trail

11801

11378

78   Canyon

HONDO   San Cristobal
Canyon
San   Cristobal   4.6   Trail

11802

11600

57

TH

10106

Cow
Lake   113

11200

10400   11737   12102

WILDERNESS   12115   1197

10683   12000   Lobo
Peak

11800

AREA   Perra   11765   Yerba
Lobo Creek   Peak

11004   1083

Legend

TH	Trailhead
▲	Campground
—	Trail
—	Other Area Trail
9760	Elevation
• **1.7** •	Trail Miles
/#/	Trail Number
—	Stream or River

North

↑

Gallina
Peak
10887

Wheeler Peak Wilderness

12. WILLIAMS LAKE (CNF #62)

To find the trail, walk down the hill and past the Bavarian Restaurant to the Kachina Chairlift and Phoenix Restaurant where you will see signs to the trail. Walk along the Rio Hondo, then bear left. The trail winds through a meadow and then across a boulder field and into the woods. It traverses another boulder field which leads to the lake. You can walk around the lake or continue up the trail to the left (east) that goes to Wheeler Peak. The hike to the lake is about 2 miles and takes an hour or more. This is a popular trail, especially on the weekends.

WILLIAMS LAKE

FULL MOON HIKE TO WILLIAMS LAKE

During the summer, Mayor Neal King leads monthly full moon hikes to Williams Lake. The hikes began several years ago, when members of the Taos Ski Valley Chamber of Commerce suggested the idea as another way to bring people up to enjoy the mountains in the summer. Taos Ski Valley Mayor Neal King leads the hikes with obvious enjoyment. He can be seen along the trail helping to direct hikers to the right path. Everyone walks at their own pace. The group can become spread out with the faster hikers so far ahead that their

LENGTH: 4-miles roundtrip to lake and back

DIFFICULTY: Moderate

ELEVATION: Begins at 10,200 feet. Williams Lake is at 11,040 feet.

HIGHLIGHTS: Blue columbine in the summer months, scenic lake, views of Wheeler Peak

DIRECTIONS: From Taos Plaza, go north on Paseo del Pueblo (US 64) approximately 4 miles. Turn right at the Ski Valley Road (NM 150). Take this road through Arroyo Seco and bear left at the old school. Continue up to Taos Ski Valley, stay left and drive into the upper parking lots. Go up Twining Road and follow the dirt road for 2 miles. There are several switchbacks that bring you to the parking lot at Deer Lane. Walk down the hill, past the Bavarian and uphill past the chairlift. Watch for the trail signs.

flashlights are not visible. The experience is surprisingly quiet, and you might feel like you are alone on the trail at times. The trail is 2-miles long one-way, and it can take an hour or more to reach the lake.

After arriving at the lake, people sit down to wait for the full moon to rise over Wheeler Peak. As the moon rises, it casts a bright glow over the lake's surface. "I really enjoy the look on peoples' faces when they see the moon starting to light up the peaks," says Mayor King.

A brisk hike up the hill may warm you, but at the lake, you will begin to cool down. It is often cold with a slight breeze. When I did the hike, I wore all my layers, including fleece, wind jacket, and gloves and wished for a hat and a thermos of hot chocolate.

On the hike down, it is quiet and the moon lights the trail, so you can see well even without a flashlight. It is a great time to listen carefully and enjoy the forest.

USING ALL YOUR SENSES

Night hiking is different from day hiking because you can't see as well and need to tune in to your other senses to notice everything happening around you. Local hiker Erica Collins notes that you might be chatting while walking during the day, but the night encourages quiet reflection and heightened awareness.

According to Francisco Cortez, wildlife program manager with the Carson National Forest, both big game animals and predators are likely to be most active at night. These animals have adapted to human presence and stay away from the trails and sleep during the day. At night, the animals wake and seek food and water. Cortez says that flashlights will likely warn wildlife of the approach of humans and an actual encounter will be quite rare.

It is more likely that you will hear animals such as owls, elk, and coyote nearby. "Sharpen up your other senses - your nose and hearing," says Cortez.

Be on the lookout for wildlife near the trail. If you see a pair of red eyes reflected in your flashlight, stop and give the animal time to escape the area.

To bring: Flashlight or head lamp, water, snacks, hot beverage

To wear: Inner layer like synthetic or silk, long pants, fleece or other warm layer, outer wind- and water- proof shell, gloves and hat. Sturdy hiking boots are recommended.

Schedule: The hikes are usually held June - September, although sometimes the June hike is canceled due to snow. The start time is typically around 8 p.m., but call (575) 776-1413 or visit www.taosskivalley.com for exact times. Dogs on a leash are welcomed. The hike is free.

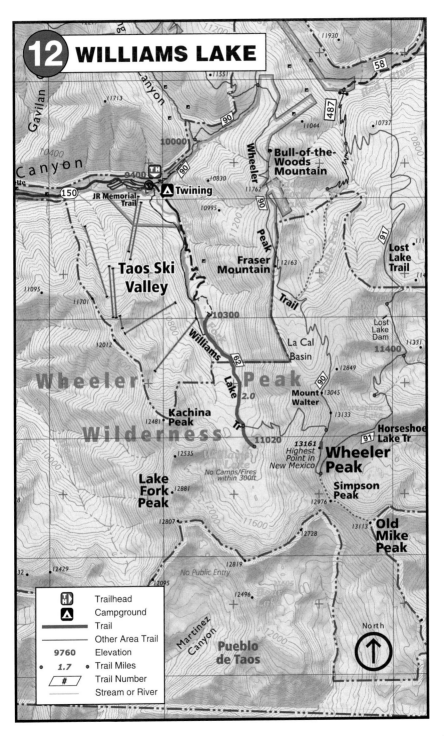

13. WHEELER PEAK (CNF #67)

WHEELER PEAK, STORM APPROACHING

LENGTH: Just under 10-miles roundtrip

DIFFICULTY: Portion of the hike to Williams Lake is moderate; the remaining section to the peak is difficult.

ELEVATION: The hike begins at 10,200 feet and ends at 13,161 feet – the highest point in New Mexico.

HIGHLIGHTS: Wildflowers in summer, views from Wheeler Peak

DIRECTIONS: From Taos Plaza, go north on Paseo del Pueblo (US 64) approximately 4 miles. Turn right at the Ski Valley Road (NM 150). Take this road through Arroyo Seco and bear left at the old school. Continue up to Taos Ski Valley, stay left and drive into the upper parking lots. Go up Twining Road and follow the dirt road for 2 miles. There are several switchbacks that bring you to the parking lot at Deer Lane. Walk down the hill, past the Bavarian and uphill past the chairlift. Watch for the trail signs.

The first section of the hike to Williams Lake is popular for good reason. It is a pleasant path through the spruce and fir trees. A gradual climb brings you through a boulder field to the lake. In the summer, there are wildflowers, including the huge blue and white columbine and the more unusual purple parry primrose. It takes about an hour to cover this part of the hike.

The trail to the peak begins just before reaching the lake. Veer left at the trail sign and continue to hike gradually uphill through the woods. Soon the trail emerges from the forest into a more open area above tree line. The trail is composed of a series of gradual switchbacks that take you higher. Below, Williams Lake is visible. Ahead you can see the ridge that connects Mount Walter and Wheeler Peak. The trail that begins on Bull-of-the-Woods travels along this ridge. Bighorn sheep are often seen in the area above tree line.

This open area is a good place to begin to notice the weather. In the summer, quite often a storm will develop in the mid-afternoon.

After reaching the ridge, the views open up dramatically to the north and east. Horseshoe Lake and Lost Lake are visible below. A short rolling section of trail on the ridge brings you to the peak. There is a plaque and a summit register containing a very full log of signatures from people reaching the top.

The hike takes about four hours to the top and three hours for the return, covering approximately 10 miles.

Trail improvement: In 2011 a Forest Service crew from Gallatin National Forest began work to improve the steep trail between the lake and the peak. They were joined by local Carson National Forest employees. Craig Saum with Trails, Wilderness and Recreation for the Carson reports, "The entire route from Williams Lake up to the peak has been completed. The trail is a much more pleasant hike with the same enormous payoff in 360-degree views." The new trail has been designed to minimize erosion and create the most sustainable trail possible. The trail work included clearing dead trees, providing trail treads, and building up segments of loose scree with rock and retaining walls to provide firmer footing. The Forest Service is asking hikers to stay on the new, improved trail to reduce the chances of erosion and hillside scarring and to help prevent loose rock from being kicked free and falling on hikers below.

History: The peak is named after Major George Wheeler of the U.S. Army who helped map this area for 10 years in the 1870s. Before 1948, it was believed that Truchas Peaks were taller than Wheeler. Harold Walter proved that Wheeler Peak was higher. He began calling a hump in the ridge Mount Walter, and it was officially so named in 1958, after his death.

Altitude: This hike begins above 10,000 feet. Although the first section to Williams Lake is not too steep, it is important to remember that you are already far above sea level, especially if you are a beginning hiker or a visitor to the area. As you continue above the lake, be sure to monitor yourself and the people with you for signs of altitude sickness, including headache, fatigue, and upset stomach. If anyone in your party experiences these symptoms, consider returning to lower elevation, resting and hydrating.

Weather: In the summer, many days will begin sunny and clear and gradually cloud up. A storm can approach from any direction. You need to be particularly alert for low dark clouds and white walls that may contain heavy rain or hail moving your way. At the first sign of lightning or thunder, it is advisable to move lower, off the exposed areas above tree line.

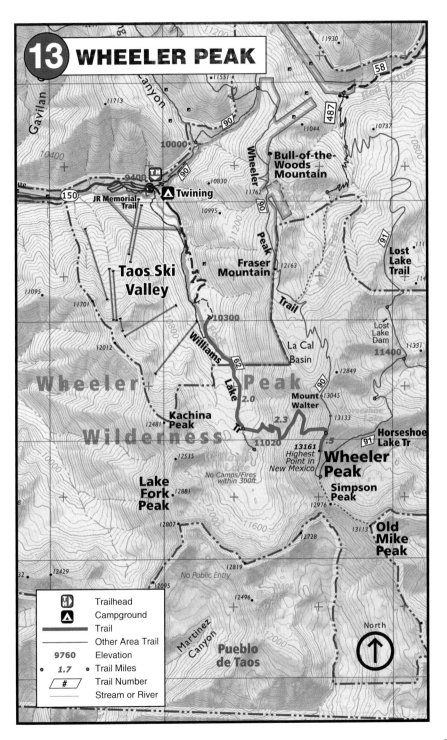

13 WHEELER PEAK

58

11930

Gavilan

Canyon

11551

11713

90

487

11044

10737

10000

10400

Wheeler

Bull-of-the-Woods Mountain

10800

9400

90

TH

Twining

150

JR Memorial Trail

10830

11762

10995

90

Peak

10400

Lost Lake Trail

111

11095

Taos Ski Valley

11701

10300

11020

Fraser Mountain

12163

Trail

114

12012

10800

Williams

62

La Cal Basin

Lost Lake Dam

11400

11331

Wheeler

Peak

2.0

12849

Mount Walter

13045

90

Kachina Peak

12481

Lake Tr

2.3

13133

13161
Highest Point in New Mexico

.5

Wheeler Peak

Horseshoe Lake Tr

91

Wilderness

12535

Williams

No Camps/Fires within 300ft

Simpson Peak

Lake Fork Peak

12881

12976

Old Mike Peak

12807

12000

11600

12728

13113

12429

12819

No Public Entry

12095

12496

North

Martinez Canyon

Pueblo de Taos

12000

Legend:

TH	Trailhead
▲	Campground
——	Trail
------	Other Area Trail
9760	Elevation
• 1.7 •	Trail Miles
/#/	Trail Number
~~	Stream or River

14. BULL-OF-THE-WOODS MEADOW (BULL-OF-THE-WOODS/WHEELER PEAK TRAIL #90)

BULL-OF-THE-WOODS MEADOW

After the monsoon rains begin (usually in July) an explosion of wildflowers can be seen in the high country near Taos. Trails near the Taos Ski Valley provide many opportunities to see flowers and enjoy the shady forests along the Rio Hondo. One particularly scenic hike is the Bull-of-the-Woods Trail, which follows a branch of the Rio Hondo. After a moderate climb of about 2 miles, hikers reach the Bull-of-the-Woods Meadow, a lovely place for a summer picnic.

The first section of trail is known as Bull-of-the-Woods, although it is actually the start of the Wheeler Peak Trail #90 in the Carson National Forest.

LENGTH: 4-miles roundtrip

DIFFICULTY: Mostly moderate

ELEVATION: Begins at 9,400 feet, ends at 10,900 feet.

HIGHLIGHTS: Hike near the Rio Hondo, wildflowers in summer, beautiful meadow

DIRECTIONS: From Taos Plaza, go north on Paseo del Pueblo (US 64) approximately 4 miles. Turn right at the Ski Valley Road (NM 150). Take this road through Arroyo Seco and bear left at the old school. Continue up to Taos Ski Valley, stay left and drive into the upper parking lots. The trailhead is located next to the parking lot or a short distance up Twining Road, if the area is still under construction. It is a total of 20 miles from the center of town and 10 miles from the Arroyo Seco post office. There is a bathroom facility at the trailhead.

The first section of the trail is the steepest part of the hike and follows the East Fork of the Rio Hondo. There are springs that cross the trail, creating the perfect environment for wildflowers, including the huge blue columbine, along with wild rose and geranium, purple chiming bells, magenta shooting stars, red Indian paintbrush, and pink little elephants.

The trail levels off and then crosses the river on a log bridge. At the 1-mile point, there is a sign indicating the turn for Long Canyon. Continue up the hill a bit farther and follow the Bull-of-the-Woods Trail as it turns left. A moderately steep section through the aspen and evergreens follows. Off to the right are several small meadows, and the river can be heard below. Views back to ski valley begin to open up here.

Follow the path until the conjunction with trails to Gold Hill and Wheeler Peak. Continue straight ahead to the Bull-of-the-Woods Meadow. Total distance from the trailhead is about 2 miles and elevation gain is approximately 1,500 feet. Look for the small pond off to the right near the trail conjunction. A spring runs through the meadow, which is full of shooting stars and many other wildflowers. This is a beautiful spot for lunch, with views of Bull-of-the-Woods Mountain to the south.

There is a yurt at the meadow run by the Southwest Nordic Center. The yurt was built in 1999, but 2014 was the first year that it was available to rent during the summer months. The price ranges from $75-$100 per night, and it can accommodate up to 10 people. For more information, call (575) 758-4761, or visit www.SouthwestNordicCenter.com.

To hike to Gold Hill, return to the trail and head north along Gold Hill Trail #64 for an additional almost 4 miles to reach the top at 12,711 feet. Wheeler Peak can be accessed by heading south an additional 6 miles to the summit at 13,161 feet. Both of these destinations include more difficult sections and travel into exposed areas above tree line.

Wildlife: The areas near the Rio Hondo attract wildlife, including elk, deer, bear, migratory birds, and grouse. However, these animals move away from the trail during the day to avoid humans, so you may not see them frequently. Heading higher onto the ridges and open meadows, it is likely that hikers will encounter small mammals such as marmots, chipmunks, squirrels, and pika. Bigger animals including elk, deer, and especially bighorn sheep are sometimes seen in the higher areas.

Weather: The ski valley is usually several degrees cooler than town. Even cooler temperatures and windy conditions can be encountered as you move higher. By mid-summer, there is often a pattern of clear mornings followed by thunderstorms in the afternoons.

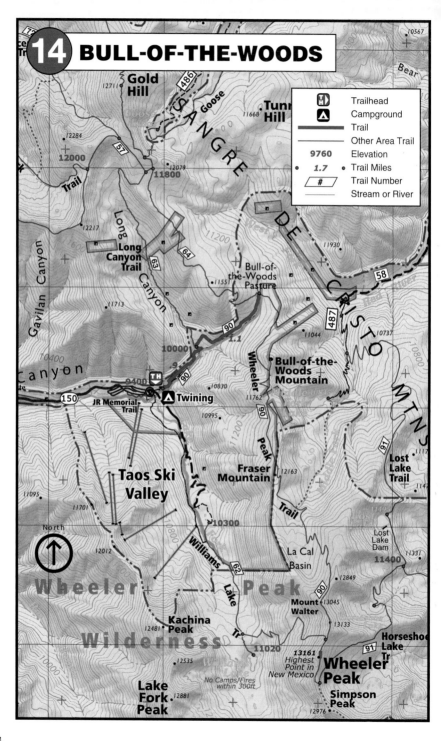

14 BULL-OF-THE-WOODS

Map Legend:

Ⓗ	Trailhead
▲	Campground
▬▬▬	Trail
────	Other Area Trail
9760	Elevation
1.7 ●	Trail Miles
⟋#⟍	Trail Number
────	Stream or River

Gold Hill

12711

Goose

Tunn Hill

11668

Bear

10567

SANGRE

486

12284

57

12000

12079

11800

DE

West

11200

11930

12217

Long Canyon Trail

Long Canyon

63

64

Bull-of-the-Woods Pasture

1155

58

CRISTO

Gavilan Canyon

11713

90

487

11044

10737

10000

1.1

Canyon

10400

.9

Wheeler

Bull-of-the-Woods Mountain

MTNS

150

TH

90

10830

Twining

Peak

91

JR Memorial Trail

11762

90

Lost Lake Trail

10995

1117

12000

1147

Taos Ski Valley

11095

11701

Fraser Mountain

12163

Trail

Lost Lake Dam

1331

12012

North

10300

Williams

La Cal Basin

11400

10800

Lake

62

12849

90

Mount Walter

13045

Wheeler

Peak

Kachina Peak

12481

13133

Horseshoe Lake Tr

Wilderness

12535

Tr

11020

91

10000

13161 Highest Point in New Mexico

Wheeler Peak

Lake Fork Peak

12881

No Camps/Fires within 300ft

Simpson Peak

12976

Latir Peak Wilderness

Latir Peak Wilderness is 20,000 acres and was designated as a wilderness area in 1980. It is one of 25 areas in New Mexico with this protection. The original Wilderness Act was signed Sept. 3, 1964 and protected 9 million acres in 13 states. Areas which are protected as wilderness create opportunities for solitude and recreation. They are generally more wild and less maintained than other areas of the forest. No motorized vehicles or bikes are allowed. Cabresto Lake is the gateway to the Latir Peak Wilderness.

15. LAKE FORK TO HEART LAKE (CNF #82)

HEART LAKE

LENGTH: Approximately 9-miles roundtrip

DIFFICULTY: Generally moderate, but due to its length, a challenging hike

ELEVATION: Begins at 9,200 feet, ends at approximately 11,500 feet.

HIGHLIGHTS: Starts at Cabresto Lake and ends at Heart Lake.

DIRECTIONS: To reach the Heart Lake Trailhead, drive north from Taos Plaza about 24 miles on Paseo del Pueblo (becomes NM 522). Turn right onto NM 38 in Questa. Turn left in 0.2 miles onto NM 563. If you miss the turn, go another half mile and turn left onto North Kiowa at the Cabresto Lake sign. From North Kiowa, go north, then west to the stop sign and turn right. Travel another 2 miles and veer right at Forest Road 134. After 3 miles, turn left onto Forest Road 134A for the climb up the 2 miles to Cabresto Lake. A high clearance vehicle works best for the last section, which is steep and rutted at times. Park near the bathroom facility. The hike begins to the left of Cabresto Lake.

Heart Lake is set in the solitude of the Latir Peak Wilderness. The trail to Heart Lake follows a crystal clear creek and climbs up to meadows full of blooming wildflowers and views of the peaks and mesas above.

The Lake Fork Trail (Carson National Forest #82) begins at beautiful blue-green Cabresto Lake, located at 9,200 feet. Walk along the north edge of the lake for a mile and cross into the wilderness. The trail follows Lake Fork Creek into the woods. Climb up along the creek, amid hillsides of lavender asters and deep purple bellflowers during the summer months. After just over 2 miles, turn right at the trail sign and cross Lake Fork Creek. Here a steady climb begins, following several switchbacks in a forest of aspen, spruce, and pine trees. Passing through several small meadows, the trail continues for 1.7 miles until the left turn to Heart Lake at the trail sign.

A short final ascent through an alpine meadow leads to serene Heart Lake, under treeless peaks, with views of Latir Mesa. Walk across the stone steps to reach the lake. Surrounded by a dense forest of spruce and pine, the lake is a soft, dark green. If you arrive early enough in the day, Heart Lake is a peaceful spot for lunch. In the summer months, watch for afternoon thunderstorms moving in from the east and south. Trails continue from the lake to Latir Mesa and Cabresto Peak. Total distance to Heart Lake is approximately 4.5 miles, and elevation gain is 2,300 feet. Although generally a moderate climb, the length of the trail and the high altitude make this a challenging hike.

Wildlife: Many birds can be heard in the forest. I've seen several northern flickers and Steller's jays. Near Cabresto Lake, I saw a blue-crested bird that may have been a belted kingfisher. The kingfisher can be seen near water hunting for small fish. According to Francisco Cortez, wildlife program manager with the Carson National Forest (CNF), other birds that live here include the golden eagle, Clark's nutcracker, and blue-winged teal duck. Also present in the forest are deer, elk, and bear. At higher elevations, near Heart Lake, bighorn sheep might be seen. Cortez says that there are brook trout and Snake River fine-spotted cutthroat trout in Cabresto Lake, where fishing is allowed.

Trail work: Recently a crew from the CNF worked on the Lake Fork Trail and nearby Bull Creek Fork Trail. The crew installed new signs and cleared the trail of fallen trees and brush to improve the hiking experience. The Carson National Forest tries to prioritize trail work based on the observations from CNF staff and input from the public.

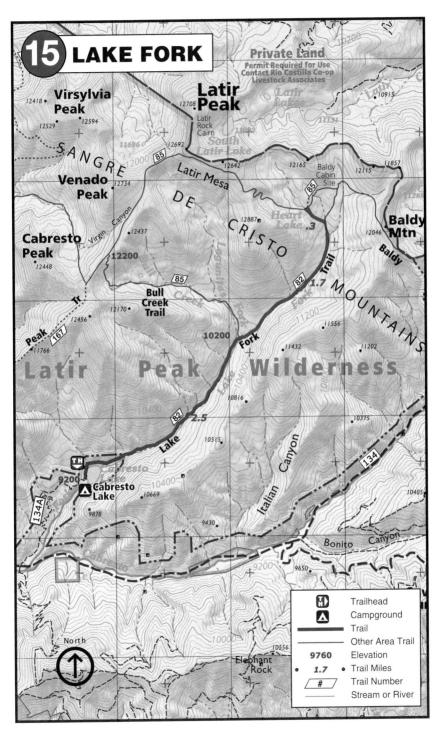

Southwest:

RIO GRANDE &
TAOS VALLEY OVERLOOK

Southwest

The hikes near the Rio Grande are great to do in the spring, winter and fall, or in the early morning during summer as it can get quite hot here in the day in summer. You might see bighorn sheep, bald eagles, hawks or other wildlife as you walk among the low-growing sage.

RIO GRANDE GORGE BRIDGE AND MOUNTAIN VIEW

16. RIO GRANDE WEST RIM - NORTH

RIO GRANDE GORGE FROM THE WEST

LENGTH: Over 9-miles from north to south one way; 3-miles roundtrip to the wash

DIFFICULTY: Easy, a flat hike

ELEVATION: Approximately 6,900 feet

HIGHLIGHTS: Desert terrain, views of the Rio Grande

DIRECTIONS: From Taos Plaza, go north on Paseo del Pueblo for 4 miles. Turn left at the signal at the intersection with US 64 and go west 7 miles. Cross the bridge and turn left at the rest stop immediately west of the bridge. There is a well-maintained bathroom and water available here. The BLM recommends that you place any valuable items, such as cameras, etc., out of sight to reduce the risk of car break-ins.

You can go as long as you like on the path, which follows the west rim of the Rio Grande. The entire trail is 9 miles each way. Mountain bikes are allowed here as well. The trail comes close to the gorge at times and then veers further away. The area is covered with black lava rocks – remnants of the volcanic past.

This is a great hike to begin the spring season. It is relatively level, with a few gently rolling sections, and offers great views of Taos Mountain and El Salto to the east. By summer, it is advisable to do the hike early in the day, before it gets too hot because there is little shade. The vegetation includes low-growing sage and a few juniper trees. An afternoon storm may roll in across the mesa. Usually there is some warning, such as a low dark cloud coming your way or the far off sound of thunder, but it is hard to judge the distance and the speed of the storm, so it is best to turn back toward the trail-head as soon as you notice the approach of a possible storm. Sunset is a beautiful and cool time to be on the trail. Nowhere is "the big sky of Taos" more evident. It can be windy at times and the sheer aloneness of the mesa can be a bit daunting, until you fall into the pleasant rhythm of walking.

Look down into the gorge and you will see the river. You may be lucky enough to see a herd of bighorn sheep on the floor of the canyon or on the rocky slopes on the east side of the gorge. Coyote, fox, and rabbit are among the animals here. Deer and elk are in the area, but less often seen.

Birds of prey such as falcons, hawks, and eagles nest on the steep walls of the gorge. Great horned owls have been sighted here as well. A variety of birds migrate through the area, including cliff swallows, which can be seen diving into the canyon. Sage and Brewer's sparrows that depend on the sage environment can be seen nesting in bushes and grass near the edge. Because there are so many birds in the area, you may wish to bring a bird identification book and a pair of binoculars.

There are snakes in this desert environment, although they generally stay hidden. The only poisonous snake is the prairie rattlesnake, identifiable by its brown and white diamond pattern and rattle. If you see a snake on the trail, you can back up and let the snake escape, and that will likely be the end of your encounter. According to the staff at BLM, letting the snake have the right of way and giving it plenty of room is always the smart choice. Valerie Williams, wildlife biologist for the BLM, notes that snakes are an important part of the desert ecosystem, controlling rodents and providing food for birds of prey. They should be left alone, never killed or disturbed.

Rafting season is spring through early summer – so you may see rafters on this section of the Rio Grande, known as the Taos Box, during this time of year.

Destinations:

Overlook – By walking about 15-20 minutes, you can reach an overlook area with a bench.

The Wash – If you continue walking for a total of more than 40 minutes, you will come to some trail markers off to your left. A few feet beyond the markers, you will see a depression in the ground covered with large black volcanic boulders. In a wet year, there will be little ponds in the area.

The Point – Another 30 minutes or more beyond the wash, you will reach a dramatic point with a lone bush to mark the area. There are good views into the gorge from this point.

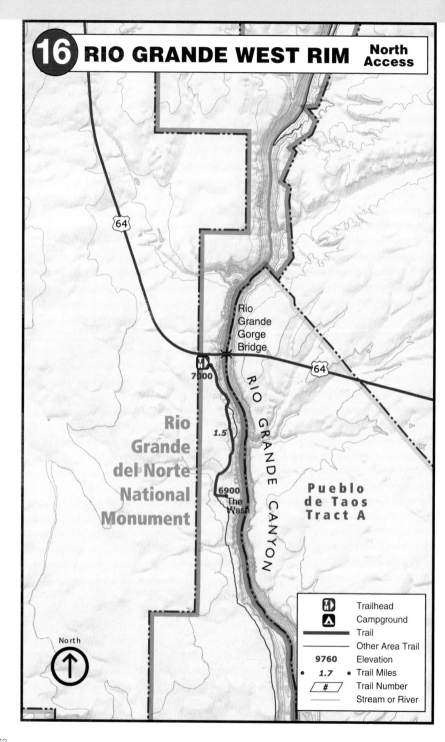

16 RIO GRANDE WEST RIM North Access

Rio Grande Gorge Bridge

7000

Rio Grande del Norte National Monument

1.5

6900
The Wash

RIO GRANDE CANYON

Pueblo de Taos Tract A

North

🅗	Trailhead
🅐	Campground
▬	Trail
—	Other Area Trail
9760	Elevation
• *1.7* •	Trail Miles
#	Trail Number
—	Stream or River

17. RIO GRANDE GORGE RIM - SOUTH

VIEW FROM THE WEST RIM OF THE RIO GRANDE GORGE

LENGTH: More than 9 miles one way, about 3-miles roundtrip to powerline

DIFFICULTY: Easy to moderate

ELEVATION: Approximately 6,800 feet

HIGHLIGHTS: Arroyos that empty into the Rio Grande, views of the river, bald eagles in winter

DIRECTIONS: From Taos Plaza, go north 4 miles on Paseo del Pueblo to the intersection of US 64 and the Ski Valley Road. Turn left at the traffic signal and drive west 7 miles to the Gorge bridge. Shortly after the bridge, turn left on the West Rim Road and drive just over 8 miles to the split at the stop sign – go left toward Pilar. There is a dirt road that goes directly to the trailhead. Look for the small trail sign to your left as you enter the Orilla Verde area. Additional trailhead parking is to the right of the road, before the descent toward the Taos Junction Bridge. This area can also be reached by going south of town on NM 68 to Pilar and turning north onto NM 570. Follow the road to the Taos Junction Bridge and climb up the dirt road with its tight switchbacks to reach the trailhead.

Although many people know about the northern trailhead, which is located just west of the Rio Grande Gorge Bridge at the rest stop, there is also a lesser-known way to begin this hike. If you drive on and turn left toward Pilar and Ojo Caliente, you can reach the south end of the Rio Grande West Rim Trail. The quiet and views into the gorge are worth the few extra miles.

West Rim – South approach: This area is known as Orilla Verde, referring to the green strip of life along the Rio Grande. Begin the hike either by turning left at the "trail" sign onto a dirt road when you enter the Orilla Verde area or by continuing on to the parking area just to the right of the road. If you park in the lot near the road, follow the trail signs that lead over the mesa. The first part of the path dips down into a protected basin, a welcome escape from the wind that can be present at some times of year. The trail passes through several arroyos on their way to drain into the Rio Grande. After about a mile, there is a series of bluffs that offer an amazing view into the gorge. To the south, the gorge widens and the river is visible and audible down below. The dramatic cliffs are lava flows exposed by the rift in the earth created by the North American continent pulling apart. The mesa is covered with sage and other low-growing plants.

Dead Cholla: From the same trailhead, you can access the Dead Cholla trail. A cholla is a spiny tree-like cactus found in the area that generally grows to between 3 and 4 feet tall. The path descends gently part way into the gorge. There are several bench-like areas that jut out and make good places to stop and look down to the river. After a distance, the road to Taos Junction Bridge is visible below.

Wildlife: According to Valerie Williams, BLM wildlife biologist, bald eagles winter here and can be seen between October and March. I've also seen red-tailed hawks. Herds of bighorn sheep are often spotted along the trail near the edge of the gorge. Williams says that the Rocky Mountain Bighorn Sheep had disappeared from this area and was reintroduced in 2006 through a partnership between the BLM, the Taos Pueblo, and New Mexico Department of Game and Fish. A herd of 23 bighorn sheep were relocated by the Pueblo from the Wheeler Peak area. The following year, an additional 25 sheep were relocated here. The herd is thriving, currently estimated to be more than 100. Other animals that might be seen include mule deer, gray fox, long tail weasel, cottontail rabbit, and coyote. Mountain lions are also present, but not often seen. Along the bottom of the gorge, river otter, which was also reintroduced, can be spotted with binoculars.

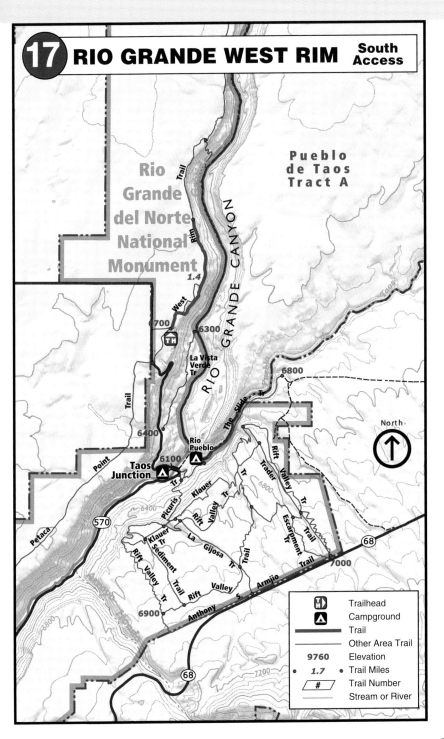

17 RIO GRANDE WEST RIM South Access

Rio Grande del Norte National Monument

Pueblo de Taos Tract A

RIO GRANDE CANYON

Rim Trail

1.4

West Trail

6700

6300

La Vista Verde Tr

6800

The Slide Tr

Trail

6400

Point Trail

Rio Pueblo

Taos Junction

6100

Picuris Tr

Klauer Tr

Rift Valley Tr

Trader Tr

Rift Valley Tr

6800

Escarpment Tr

68

Klauer Tr

La Gijosa Tr

Sediment Trail

570

Petaca

Rift Valley Tr

7000

Rift Valley

Anthony S. Armijo Trail

6400

6900

6800

68

7200

Legend

- 🚻 Trailhead
- ⛺ Campground
- ▬▬ Trail
- ---- Other Area Trail
- **9760** Elevation
- ● *1.7* ● Trail Miles
- ⬦ *#* Trail Number
- ～～ Stream or River

North ↑

75

18. LA SENDA DEL MEDIO

VIEWS FROM LA SENDA DEL MEDIO

LENGTH: 5-miles roundtrip

DIFFICULTY: Easy to moderate

ELEVATION: Approximately 6,000 feet

HIGHLIGHTS: Views of the Rio Grande, lava cliffs

DIRECTIONS: From Taos Plaza, drive south on Paseo del Pueblo Sur (NM 68) about 30 minutes and 17 miles to the Rio Grande Gorge Visitor Center. From the center, cross NM 68 and head north on NM 570, which parallels the Rio Grande, for just over a mile to the Pilar Campground. Park in the day use area.

You can return the same way, or if you are feeling adventurous, you can continue north on NM 570 another five miles to the Taos Junction Bridge. After crossing the bridge, there are a series of switchbacks on the steep dirt road that climb up to the level of the gorge rim. Pass by the Taos Junction Campground and two trailheads, and the road arrives at the West Rim Road. It is just over 8 miles to US 64, where you will turn right and cross the Rio Grande Gorge Bridge. An additional 7 miles will bring you to the intersection of US 64 and NM 150 (Ski Valley Road). Turn right on Paseo del Pueblo and drive 4 miles south to the Plaza.

This is a relatively new trail, built by the Rocky Mountain Youth Corps, working with the BLM. La Senda del Medio (the Middle Path) connects the five campgrounds located north of Pilar on NM 570. It is a spectacular hike down in the gorge surrounded by sheer cliffs and full of history.

The hike begins at the Pilar Campground and ends at the Petaca area. At first the terrain is wide open, surrounded by sage and a few juniper trees. The path winds back away from NM 570 in between rocky lava walls, with the cliffs of the gorge dominating views on both sides. The trail goes through rolling hills, climbing on rocky steps and descending gradually into valleys. There are glimpses of the Rio Grande across the road.

A sign marks each of the trail spurs that lead to the in-between campground – Rio Bravo, Arroyo Hondo, and Lone Juniper. In the spring, yellow flowers bloom on the yucca.

There are often signs of coyote on the trail. Randy Roch, lower gorge manager for the BLM, points out that there is variety of wildlife that might be seen on the trail – including bighorn sheep, lizards, deer and elk, as well as many birds. The gorge is a migratory path for birds; hawks and both bald and golden eagles have been spotted. Although they are in the area, it is rare to see black bear, bobcat, and mountain lion. Roch said that there are a variety of snakes – with rattlers being rare. He said he has more often seen bull snakes, which resemble rattlers, but are non-venomous.

Rio Grande Gorge Visitor Center: At the Rio Grande Gorge Visitor Center, there are maps, books, and a knowledgeable staff. It is open all year-round, from 10 a.m. to 2 p.m. daily – November to mid-April, and from 8:30 a.m. to 4:30 p.m. the rest of the year. Phone number is (575) 751-4899. You can get information about current trail and river conditions. Even in the offseason, there is a steady stream of visitors in the center, talking to the staff and looking over the display of Rio Grande paintings and photos. After mid-April, the number of visitors rises dramatically as the rafting season begins.

History: There is evidence of Native American habitation and of an early travel corridor for the Spanish – the Camino Real. When Americans arrived in the 1800s, they used the gorge as a stagecoach route and later for the railroad. Ruins of a possible stagecoach stop are located near the Taos Junction Bridge.

This area was part of a state park from 1959 until the land was transferred to the BLM in 1990. The visitor center was built in 1996 and has been providing information and serving as a parking area and beginning point for rafters since that time. There is a meeting room that is used for environmental education and guided hikes often begin here.

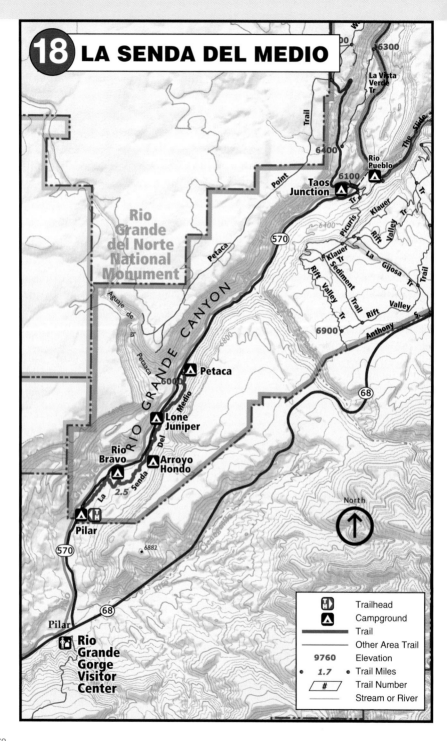

18 LA SENDA DEL MEDIO

6300

La Vista
Verde
Tr

Trail

6400

Rio
Pueblo

Point

6100

Taos
Junction

Tr

570

Picuris Tr

Klauer Tr

Rift Valley Tr

Rio
Grande
del Norte
National
Monument

Petaca

Klauer
Tr

Sediment Trail

La Gijosa Tr

Valley

Aguaje de la

Rift Valley Tr

Rift

Valley

6900

Anthony

S.

6800

RIO GRANDE CANYON

Petaca

6000

Petaca

68

Del Medio

Lone
Juniper

Rio
Bravo

Arroyo
Hondo

2.5 Senda

La

North

Pilar

570

6882

68

Pilar

Rio
Grande
Gorge
Visitor
Center

Trailhead	
Campground	
⎯⎯⎯	Trail
—	Other Area Trail
9760	Elevation
• 1.7 •	Trail Miles
#	Trail Number
⎯⎯	Stream or River

19. TAOS VALLEY OVERLOOK: TRADER'S TRAIL AND RIFT VALLEY

TRAIL MARKER ALONG THE RIO GRANDE GORGE

LENGTH: Trader's Trail is just over 3-miles roundtrip, Rift Valley 6-miles roundtrip

DIFFICULTY: Easy to moderate

ELEVATION: Begins at 7,000 feet and drops near the gorge

HIGHLIGHTS: Sage and juniper, views of the Rio Pueblo and Rio Grande

DIRECTIONS: From the Plaza, go south on Paseo del Pueblo less than 10 miles. After Stakeout Drive, continue on until you see a brown hiker sign, just past mile marker 36. The trailhead parking lot is a short distance beyond on the right.

A series of interconnected hikes begins at the Taos Valley Overlook trailhead about 15 minutes south of town. Trader's Trail is just over 1.5 miles and follows a long gradual slope down toward the Rio Grande Gorge. The trail is surrounded by low-growing sage and a few juniper trees. From near the beginning of the trail, there are glimpses of the basalt rock walls of the gorge. After about 40 minutes, you will reach an overlook point – with views of the river below and the bridge at Taos Junction to the south. Look for the bench provided by "friends of Rift Valley trail."

Trader's Trail connects with the Rift Valley, Klauer, La Gijosa, and Anthony S. Armijo trails that meander across the valley to the north and south. The Rift Valley trail to the south is a 10-mile loop that makes a great bike ride. There is also a short practice bike loop at the first right turn from Trader's Trail. This portion of the Rift Trail meanders down toward a rocky arroyo that drains into the Rio Pueblo. This section of the Rift Valley Trail eventually rejoins Trader's Trail near the overlook. Rift Valley also connects with County Road 110.

For a longer hike, head off to the left (south) on the Rift Valley Trail. Follow it as it rolls through the piñon and juniper until you reach the Escarpment Trail, which is not shown on some maps, but is a short cut to reach Klauer Trail. Turn left at the double-track Klauer path and follow it as it traverses several arroyos. Continue on near the edge of the Rio Grande Gorge until you reach the Picuris Trail, which descends into the gorge. Round trip, this hike covers almost 6 miles.

Wildlife: Valerie Williams, wildlife biologist with the BLM, says that hikers may see bighorn sheep, especially on the tribal lands across the Rio Pueblo. Deer and elk might be seen in early morning or twilight hours in drainage areas. Bald and golden eagles are cruising the rivers in search of food, along with migratory birds such as Canadian geese, mallard, wood duck, and great blue heron. The bluish pinyon jays can be seen sometimes in flocks of a few birds to 100 or more. Coyotes and rabbits are found here, and bobcats may be present but are rarely seen.

History: Much of this system of trails existed before the BLM acquired the land. According to Tami Torres, outdoor recreation planner for the BLM, the trails were named for some of the known history of the area. Rift Valley refers to the way the Rio Grande Gorge was formed. The river did not cut the gorge, as is the case with some rivers. Rather a small river beginning near Leadville, Colorado, followed a cut in the earth made by the heaving and shifting of the land. The Rio Grande Rift is a 600-mile long split in North America that has allowed the Rio Grande to run from its headwaters near Creede, Colorado through New Mexico and onto the Gulf of Mexico.

One trail is named for the Gijosa family who received the original land grant. According to local historians, the grant was made to Maria Gijosa in the early 1700s. Under Spanish law, which was more progressive than early US law, a woman could receive a land grant. Used for many years to graze sheep, the area saw periodic raids from the Comanche. Early native peoples crossed the land, and it is believed that an extension of the Camino Real trail came into Taos here. Spanish explorers, American trappers and traders, missionaries, and settlers used the trails. In 1876, the U.S. Military built the first usable wagon road along the Rio Grande to bring supplies through New Mexico to Fort Garland in Colorado.

Klauer, the long double-track section that runs parallel to the river gorge, is named after the Klauer family of Iowa that manufactured flumes and piping and produced stamped metal ceilings. They held this parcel in the 1800s, although there is no evidence that any manufacturing was done here.

Sam DesGeorges, field manager for the BLM Taos Office, says that he loves the history of the area and the way that it reminds us that the past is not separate from the present. He says there are descendants in Taos and at the Pueblo of those same families who were part of the history of this area. "The preservation of such parcels is a bridge to the past, as well as our connection to the future," says DesGeorges. The trails here were formalized, and the trailhead area was dedicated in the fall of 2009. The entire parcel is part of the Rio Grande del Norte National Monument.

Weather: This area is accessible for hiking all year-round and is most pleasant in the fall, winter, and spring. Although there will be times of snow during the winter, the area is not shaded and the snow quite often melts here quickly. More lightly traveled than other times of year, the trails offer the opportunity to observe the glistening silence of the desert in winter. As Valerie Williams says, "It is a time to enjoy the quiet and solitude and listen to the wind." Although the trails are generally accessible throughout the season, the BLM asks that bicyclists stay off the trail to avoid creating deep ruts when it is wet and muddy.

Information: For more information, call the BLM Taos Field Office at (575) 758-8851 or stop by 226 Cruz Alta Road to pick up maps. You can visit the BLM online at http://www.blm.gov/nm/st/en.html.

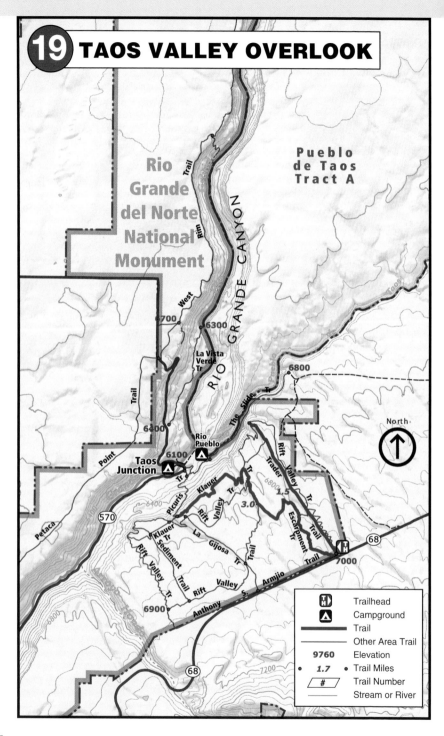

19 TAOS VALLEY OVERLOOK

Rio Grande del Norte National Monument

Pueblo de Taos Tract A

RIO GRANDE CANYON

Trail

Rim

West

700

6300

La Vista Verde Tr

The Slide Tr

6800

6400

Rio Pueblo

6100

Taos Junction

Point

Tr

Trail

Picuris

Klauer Tr

Rift Valley Tr

Trader Tr

3.0

1.7

Rift Valley Tr

Escarpment Tr

North

Petaca

570

Klauer Tr

Sediment Tr

Rift Valley Tr

La Gijosa Tr

Valley Trail

Rift Valley

Armjio S.

Trail

7000

68

6900

Anthony S.

68

7200

	Trailhead
	Campground
	Trail
	Other Area Trail
9760	Elevation
1.7	Trail Miles
#	Trail Number
	Stream or River

20. THE SLIDE TRAIL

CONFLUENCE OF THE RIO GRANDE AND RIO PUEBLO

Old 570, the perilous road leading into the canyon of the Rio Pueblo, was closed more than 20 years ago after a massive rockslide. Long-time Taoseños tell stories of taking the family pickup truck down this road in order to cross Taos Junction Bridge and get wood near Carson. They mostly remember holding their breath in fear, while driving back up along the narrow gravel road with a full load of wood, looking down over the steep cliff to the Rio Pueblo below.

After more than 57,000 pounds of basalt rock fell on the road in early 1993, the State Department of Transportation decided not to re-open it. The road became a trail overseen by the BLM,

LENGTH: 2.6-miles roundtrip

DIFFICULTY: Moderate

ELEVATION: Begins at 6,100 feet and gains 700 feet.

HIGHLIGHTS: Views of the Rio Pueblo, bighorn sheep often seen

DIRECTIONS: North approach – drive north 4 miles from the Plaza on Paseo del Pueblo to the intersection with the Ski Valley Road. Turn left onto US 64 and drive past the Rio Grande Gorge Bridge. Turn left onto the West Rim Road toward Pilar and Ojo Caliente. After about 8 miles, there is a stop sign; make a slight left and continue past the Petaca Point trailhead. The road is gravel, narrow and windy from this point on, with steep drop-offs to the Rio Grande below. Cross the Taos Junction Bridge and turn left into the Rio Pueblo Campground. There is a fee station where you can pay the $3 fee for day use. Continue up the road to the left and park near the trailhead. The entire one-way trip is about 23 miles. There are outhouse facilities at the campground.

South approach – drive south from the Plaza on Paseo del Pueblo, just over 5.5 miles. Turn right at C110, the road to the National Guard and Country Club and continue on 4 miles. Park at the dirt lot just above the rocks that close the road. This approach brings you to the top of the trail.

known as The Slide Trail. It is part of the Orilla Verde (green ribbon) trail system and can be accessed either from County Road 110, past the Klauer campus of the University of New Mexico – Taos or from the Taos Junction Bridge area.

From the Taos Junction Bridge, it is a pleasant and moderate climb up a gravel surface that is partially overgrown with grasses, sage, and willow. The rockslide section is near the bottom, and here the path narrows and climbs up and down for a short section. The trail was improved recently with the help of the Rocky Mountain Youth Corps, so that the slide section has a trail through it, rather than requiring a scramble over the boulders. The trail crosses several springs and arroyos that empty into the river.

Spring is a good time to explore the hikes near the Rio Pueblo and Rio Grande. The relatively low elevation at 6,100 feet ensures that the area gets less snow and that the snow melts faster than some of the higher elevation hikes. Later in the season it gets hot here, but during the spring the temperatures are usually moderate. The trail starts almost level with the Rio Pueblo and gradually climbs up away from the river. Views over to the Pueblo land across the river are filled with massive lava formations, so large they resemble great rocky ocean liners.

Near the top, there are vertigo-inducing views down to the river far below. It is worth noting that this hike may not be appropriate for people with a fear of heights. There are a few remnants of the old road, with an occasional post, concrete barrier, or car visible on the rocky slopes that lead to the river. The top section of the trail is the most heavily impacted by humans with graffiti and litter. Tami Torres says that the BLM has acquired 78 acres at the high end of the trail adjacent to the south side of C110, where it terminates at the jersey barriers leading into the Rio Pueblo de Taos canyon. The BLM has begun to actively manage this area to prevent dumping and is constructing a trailhead, along with picnic tables, signing and trails that connect to the Rift Valley trail system.

There are often bighorn sheep visible on both sides of the Rio Pueblo. Other animals that can be seen are lizards, deer and elk, as well as many birds. The gorge is a migratory path for birds; hawks, along with bald and golden eagles have been spotted. Although they are in the area, it is unusual to see black bear, bobcat, and mountain lion. There are a variety of snakes, with rattlesnakes being rare.

The lower trailhead is near the confluence of the Rio Pueblo and the Rio Grande. There is tremendous energy where the two come together, producing thundering rapids and sparkling spray.

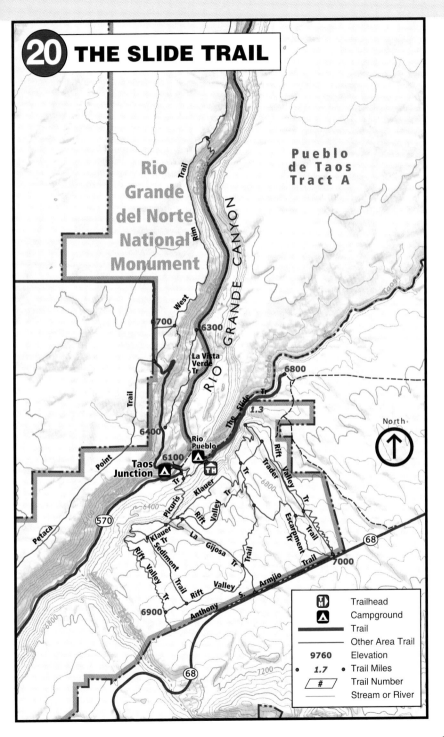

20 THE SLIDE TRAIL

Rio Grande del Norte National Monument

Pueblo de Taos Tract A

RIO GRANDE CANYON

Rim Trail

West Trail

6700

6300

La Vista Verde Tr

6800

The Slide Tr

1.3

6400

Trail

Point

Rio Pueblo

6100

TH

Taos Junction

Tr

570

Klauer Tr

Rift Valley Tr

Trader Valley Tr

6800

North

Picuris Tr

6400

Klauer Tr

La Gijosa Tr

Sediment Trail

Rift Valley Tr

Valley Trail

Escarpment Tr

Trail

68

7000

Rift Valley Tr

Rift Valley Tr

Armijo S.

Anthony

6900

6800

68

7200

Petaca

	Trailhead
	Campground
	Trail
	Other Area Trail
9760	Elevation
1.7	Trail Miles
#	Trail Number
	Stream or River

21. PICURIS TRAIL

PETROGLYPH ON PICURIS TRAIL

LENGTH: 1.5-miles roundtrip

DIFFICULTY: Moderately difficult

ELEVATION: Starts at approximately 6,100 feet and gains 600 feet

HIGHLIGHTS: Views of the Rio Grande

DIRECTIONS: From Taos Plaza, drive north 4 miles on Paseo del Pueblo to the intersection with the Ski Valley Road. Turn left onto US 64 and drive past the Rio Grande Gorge Bridge. Turn left onto the West Rim Road toward Pilar and Ojo Caliente. After about 8 miles, there is a stop sign; make a slight left and continue past the Petaca Point trailhead. From this point on, the road is gravel, narrow and windy, with steep drop-offs to the Rio Grande below. Cross the Taos Junction Bridge and turn right. Parking is available near the boat launch ramp. There is a fee station near the bathrooms where you can pay the $3 fee for day use. The entire one-way trip is about 23 miles. The trailhead is located on the other side of NM 570. An alternate approach is to drive south from Taos Plaza on Paseo del Pueblo/NM 68 to Pilar 17 miles. Turn north on NM 570 for about 6 miles and head toward the Taos Junction Bridge. The mileage from the Plaza is similar for either approach.

Picuris Trail is a short steep path, beginning near the Taos Junction Bridge and ending on the mesa above the Rio Grande. It is part of the Orilla Verde Recreation area. Tami Torres, recreation planner with the Bureau of Land Management (BLM) says, "The trail is single track, hiking only, and more primitive to protect it as a historic resource. Visitors may want to be more aware in following the trail, due to its faint and narrow tread surface. It is marked in some places with small cairns."

The hike begins at a trailhead just across NM 570 from the Taos Junction Bridge. After a few rock steps, there are a series of switchbacks through the sage, piñon, juniper, and cholla cactus. A few segments of the trail require some scrambling over the basalt rocks. There is a flat shelf mid-way up the trail that offers a good place to turn and look back toward the Rio Grande. The trail begins to climb again and at the top, joins the Klauer Trail, which is part of the Rift Valley system. Even when it is windy, this hike is more protected and is mostly calm, until the very top. Bighorn sheep are often seen near the Rio Grande.

Local historians think that this trail was used by Native Americans. There are petroglyphs in the area: pictures carved in stone by people passing through the gorge in the past. Merrill Dicks, archeologist with the BLM says that there are many rock symbols here, indicating that it is a very old trail. He says that the Taos Junction area, which is the confluence of the Rio Pueblo and the Rio Grande, has long been an important crossing point. Dicks reminds trail users that petroglyphs are an important cultural resource that should be preserved for the future. He says, "People should not climb on the boulders or do rubbings of the designs, as both cause deterioration."

Hike options: The hike can be done as a short steep up-and-down roundtrip. Another option is to begin at the Taos Valley Overlook trailhead on NM 68, south of Taos. Take the Rift Valley Trail to Klauer via Escarpment and connect to Picuris, then hike down to the Rio Grande. If you park a vehicle at each end, the hike will cover about 4 miles. For a truly epic hike, follow the path outlined above, but near the bottom of Picuris, take the new connector trail from Picuris to the Slide Trail (Old 570), off to the right. Hike up 1.3 miles on the Slide Trail to the mesa. From the top, follow C110 as it connects back to Trader's Trail and the Taos Valley Overlook trailhead.

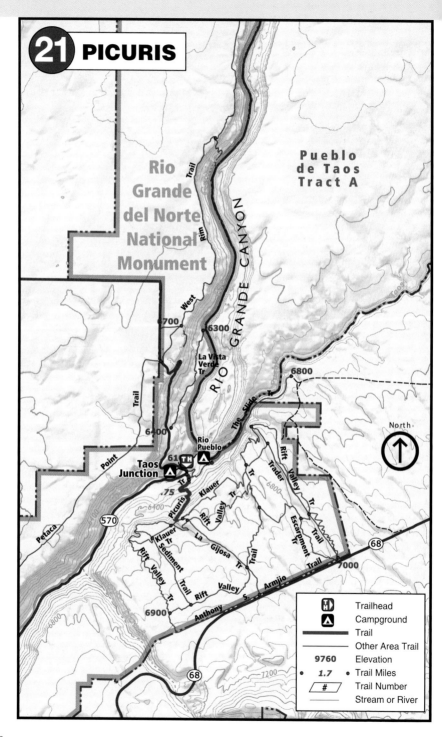

21 PICURIS

Rio Grande del Norte National Monument

Pueblo de Taos Tract A

RIO GRANDE CANYON

Trail
Rim
West
6700
6300
La Vista Verde Tr
6800
The Guide Tr
Trail
6400
Rio Pueblo
Riff Valley
Trader Tr
Point
Taos Junction
61
.75
Klauer
Tr
North
Picuris Tr
Rift Valley Tr
6800
Klauer Tr
Tr
Escarpment Tr
Trail
570
6400
Klauer Tr
Sediment
La Gijosa Tr
Trail
7000
68
Petaca
Rift Valley Trail
Tr
Rift Valley
Armijo
Trail
6900
Anthony
S
6800
7200
68

🅷	Trailhead
◮	Campground
▬▬▬	Trail
——	Other Area Trail
9760	Elevation
• *1.7* •	Trail Miles
/#/	Trail Number
——	Stream or River

22. LA VISTA VERDE

RAPIDS IN THE RIO GRANDE FROM LA VISTA VERDE

LENGTH: 2.5-miles roundtrip

DIFFICULTY: Easy

ELEVATION: 6,400 feet, relatively flat

HIGHLIGHTS: Views of the Rio Grande, petroglyphs. The best way to see petroglyphs on this hike is to go on one of the guided hikes led in the spring and summer by BLM rangers.

DIRECTIONS: From Taos Plaza, go north four miles on Paseo del Pueblo to the intersection of US 64 and the Ski Valley Road. Turn left at the traffic signal and drive west 7 miles to the Gorge bridge. Shortly after the bridge, turn left on West Rim Road and drive just over 8 miles to the stop sign. Go left toward Pilar. Follow the road as it turns to dirt and descend the switchbacks until you see La Vista Verde trailhead to the left.

La Vista Verde hike is located between the rim of the gorge and the river on a wide bench of land, just above the Taos Junction Bridge. The hike is 2.5 miles round trip over gently rolling terrain and concludes at a point overlooking the Rio Grande. In the spring there are bright red blooming cactus, known as the claret cup.

On La Vista Verde trail, there are several areas containing carved symbols left by Native American tribes, as well as Spanish travelers and others, who moved through the area. Spanish crosses can be seen near the trail. In an area farther from the path, there is a grouping of circular designs, as well as depictions of human-like figures and long flowing curves. Merrill Dicks, archeologist with the BLM, says that there are many interpretations for these symbols, but in most cases the meanings are not certain because they have been lost or held secret. According to Dicks, the long, flowing extended designs are thought to tell the story of a journey. *The Field Guide to Rock Art Symbols of the Greater Southwest* by Alex Patterson has a key to petroglyphs designs. Water, irrigation, and rainbows are among the symbols that look similar to the long, flowing designs on La Vista Verde trail. Also seen here is a symbol that shows a human-like figure that may represent the god of death.

According to Dicks, the BLM seeks to strike a balance between protecting the cultural resources of the area and making them available to visitors. He says, "The trails have been intentionally constructed in this area, so that people can experience this amazing landscape, including its cultural resources. We are charged with protecting the petroglyphs and at same time making it possible for visitors to enjoy this trail and others."

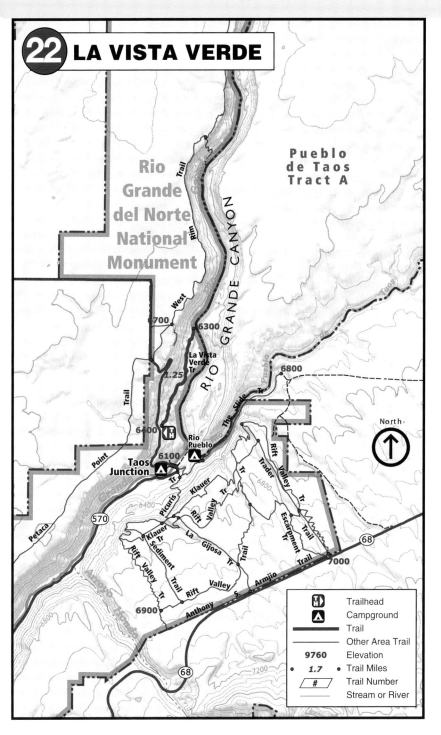

22 LA VISTA VERDE

Rio Grande del Norte National Monument

Pueblo de Taos Tract A

RIO GRANDE CANYON

Rim Trail

West Trail

6700

6300

La Vista Verde Tr

1.25

6400

6100

Rio Pueblo

6800

The Slide Tr

Taos Junction

Point Trail

570

6400

Petaca

Picuris Tr

Klauer Tr

Klauer Tr

La Valley

Rift Valley

Gijosa Tr

La Valley Trail

Sediment Trail

Rift Valley Tr

Rift Valley

Trader Valley Tr

Escarpment Tr

Trail

7000

68

Anthony S. Armijo Trail

6900

68

7200

North ↑

Legend	
🏠	Trailhead
⛺	Campground
▬▬	Trail
──	Other Area Trail
9760	Elevation
• *1.7* •	Trail Miles
/#/	Trail Number
──	Stream or River

Southeast:
TAOS CANYON & NM 518

Southeast

Taos Canyon, east of town, holds a variety of hikes, many of them following old logging roads. Also in this area are the hikes accessed from NM 518, southeast of town. Both areas are great to do during the fall, because the aspens last longer due to the relatively low elevations. Snow usually melts here earlier as well.

CLIFFS AND ASPEN ON SANTA BARBARA TRAIL

23. DEVISADERO

DEVISADERO ROCK FORMATION

LENGTH: 5-miles roundtrip

DIFFICULTY: Mostly moderate with some steeper sections

ELEVATION: Begins at approximately 7,200 feet; peak is at 8,304 feet.

HIGHLIGHTS: Spring flowers, Taos and mesa views

DIRECTIONS: From Taos Plaza, take Kit Carson (US 64) 2.8 miles to the trailhead parking lot – on your right.

A local favorite, Devisadero is on the sunny side of Taos Canyon and just under 3 miles from downtown. A variety of trails start at the trailhead parking lot, including South Boundary and Ojitos. Devisadero is an enjoyable hike in the spring, winter, and fall due to the low-growing vegetation that allows the sun to melt the snow.

To begin the hike, cross Kit Carson Road. The trail begins with an uphill section of about one-half mile to a trail marker. At the marker, you can choose to go to the right for a shorter, steeper hike to the peak, or you can go left for a flatter, longer hike through a more forested area. If you hike the short steeper section to the right, there is a sign pointing to the scar from the 1967 Vinateria fire across the highway.

At the top, there is a circle of rocks and some stone chairs, along with the trail marker, indicating the elevation. This whole hike will take between 2.5 and 3 hours, if you walk briskly. If walking more slowly or taking time to catch your breath, it will take longer to complete the loop.

If you have less time or are just getting started hiking, you might chose to do a shorter hike – just uphill about 30 to 45 minutes. In that amount of time, you will gain substantial elevation and get some fresh air and great views across the valley and mesa to beyond the Rio Grande Gorge. Several flat, rocky hilltops on the way to the peak provide good places to rest or to end a shorter hike.

This trail goes through areas of low-growing piñon and juniper trees as well as taller, more forested sections, some terraced with rocky outcroppings. Stay on the trail to avoid crossing onto private land.

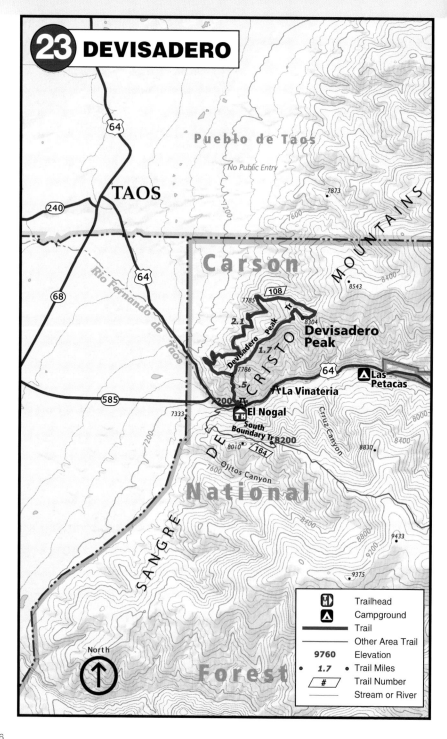

23 DEVISADERO

Pueblo de Taos

No Public Entry

TAOS

Carson

MOUNTAINS

Devisadero Peak

La Vinateria

Las Petacas

El Nogal

South Boundary Tr

Ojitos Canyon

National

Forest

Rio Fernando de Taos

Cruz Canyon

North

	Trailhead
	Campground
	Trail
	Other Area Trail
9760	Elevation
• *1.7* •	Trail Miles
#	Trail Number
	Stream or River

24. SOUTH BOUNDARY TRAIL (CNF #164)

EARLY EASTER DAISY ON SOUTH BOUNDARY

LENGTH: 22-miles one way, overlook at 1.5 miles

DIFFICULTY: Moderate to difficult

ELEVATION: Starts near 7,200 feet, overlook is at 8,200 feet.

HIGHLIGHTS: Spring and summer flowers, views of Taos, rock formations, overlooks

DIRECTIONS: From Taos Plaza, take Kit Carson (US 64) 2.8 miles east to the trailhead parking lot, on the right at the El Nogal picnic area. There is a bathroom facility that is open during the summer.

The South Boundary Trail is one of most popular hiking trails in the Carson National Forest, along with Devisadero, with which it shares a trailhead in Taos Canyon. Shady forests of piñon and juniper, along with rocky sections and overlooks with views of Taos and the surrounding mountains make this a pleasant and memorable hike.

South Boundary is also becoming well-known among mountain bikers. It is one of three Carson National Forest (CNF) trails designated as a National Recreation Trail, recognizing its local and regional significance. The trail is 22 miles in length and has a growing reputation as a challenging and scenic ride.

In the spring, little clusters of wild flowers appear, including the Early Easter Daisy. Local flower expert David Witt says that the Early Easter Daisy is "one of the first three flowers to show up along the South Boundary Trail. Also look for Slimleaf Purple Mustard and Oval Leaf Bladderpod – bright yellow flowers."

"Spring is a wake-up call for all animals," says Francisco Cortez, wildlife biologist at the CNF. Cortez points out that migratory birds, such as the hummingbird, return to the area in spring. It is breeding season for birds, and the males can be heard calling or gobbling, as is the case with the wild turkey. "Bigger animals, like bears, are waking up and coming out of hibernation. This time of year they are focused on early plants foraging," says Cortez. Reptiles, such as the southwestern fence lizard and rattlesnake, are also leaving their winter burrows.

To begin the hike, cross the bridge over the Rio Fernando. The first section is a moderate climb through the piñon and juniper trees. Stay right at the first trail division and follow a series of uphill switchbacks that become a bit steeper. At just over a mile, the trail emerges onto an open ridge with views back into Taos. Climb up through a rocky set of stairs to a high point at about 1.5 miles. Off to the left, there is an overlook that offers great views of the Rio Grande to the west and Taos Mountain to the northeast. This is a good spot to end a short hike. Total elevation gain is about 1,000 feet between the trailhead and the overlook.

Hikers who continue on will make their way through the ponderosa pine to another overlook with views of Wheeler Peak. For a long hike or ride into higher elevations, follow South Boundary for just over 13 miles to the Mondragon Canyon trailhead, located farther east on US 64. The end of the trail is accessed from Forest Road 76, for a total trail length of 22 miles. Mountain bikers riding the whole length often begin at Forest Road 76 and end at the Taos Canyon trailhead, in order to enjoy the scenic descent into Taos.

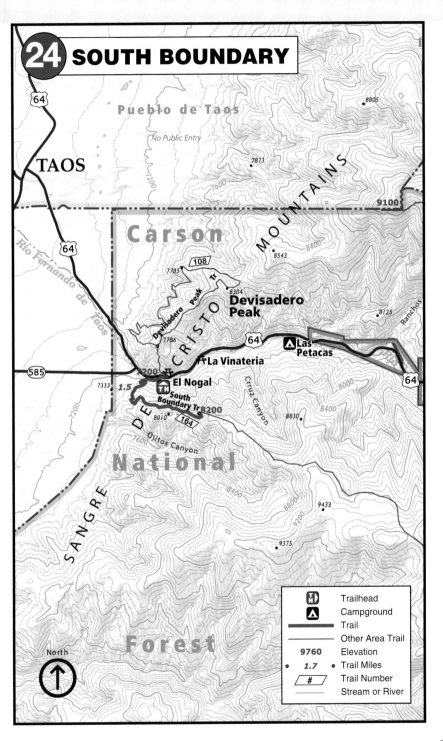

24 SOUTH BOUNDARY

64

Pueblo de Taos

No Public Entry

8805

TAOS

7873

Carson

64

Rio Fernando de Taos

108

7785

Devisadero Peak Tr

8304

Devisadero Peak

8543

8125

Ranchos

7786

64

Las Petacas

DE CRISTO

MOUNTAINS

585

7200

La Vinateria

El Nogal

South Boundary Tr 8200

164

8010

7333

1.5

Cruz Canyon

8830

8000

8400

64

Ojitos Canyon

National

8400

9433

9375

SANGRE

Forest

North

↑

🅷	Trailhead
⛺	Campground
▬▬	Trail
──	Other Area Trail
9760	Elevation
• **1.7** •	Trail Miles
#	Trail Number
──	Stream or River

25. ELLIOTT BARKER TRAIL (CNF #1)

VIEW TOWARD WHEELER FROM ELLIOTT BARKER TRAIL

Climbing high above the Moreno Valley, the Elliott Barker Trail offers spectacular views of Angel Fire and Wheeler Peak. This system of trails was built through the cooperation of a citizen group from Angel Fire and the Carson National Forest. Connecting old logging roads and animal paths, the trails provide hiking, biking, and horseback riding opportunities through the ponderosa pine and aspen forest.

LENGTH: 6- to 8-miles roundtrip to Apache Pass, depending on route

DIFFICULTY: Moderate

ELEVATION: 8,500 feet to 9,400 feet

HIGHLIGHTS: Views into Moreno Valley, wildflowers

DIRECTIONS: The trailhead is located 19.6 miles east on Kit Carson (US 64) from Taos Plaza. Go over Palo Flechado Pass. At the bottom of the hill and after mile marker 274, turn right into the trailhead. To start out from the top of the pass, park near the Palo Flechado historic sign and cross the highway to enter the trail area.

There are a variety of choices from the trailhead, which is located at approximately 8,500 feet at the bottom of Palo Flechado Pass on US 64. For a short hike and a good picnic spot, continue from the trailhead straight ahead across the meadow and through the opening in the wooden fence. A small pond is visible just ahead. Hikers who continue past the pond on this route will climb another three-quarters of a mile to meet US 64 at Palo Flechado pass. The trail continues on through a gate and turns back into the forest of pine, spruce, and aspen, climbing another 1.25 miles to reach a wide-open area known as Bull Springs Meadow. The forest here shows signs of the history of logging. Along this section, I saw the large pheasant-like bird known as the blue grouse and also some pale purple pasqueflowers. It is also possible to access the trail by parking at the Palo Flechado historic marker at the top of the pass on US 64 and crossing the road to pass through the gate.

The historic marker says that Palo Flechado means "tree pierced with arrows." It was named for either the Flecha de Palo Apache band that lived in the area in the early 1700s, or for the custom of the Taos Pueblo Indians who shot unused arrows through a tree at the pass to mark a successful buffalo hunt.

An alternate approach is to hike from the trailhead through the first meadow and turn left to cross the small creek. This route begins with a moderately steep climb over log steps until it reaches a flatter section through the forest. At the first major trail intersection, you can turn left and follow a three-quarter mile loop that returns to the trailhead for a total hike of just under a mile and a half. To continue higher, turn right and climb into the forest. There are aspen trees in this section and signs of elk. Views of Angel Fire and the Moreno Valley open to the left and the Vietnam Veteran's Memorial is visible in the valley. Back over your shoulder are views of the Wheeler Peak ridge to the north. After a total of 3 miles from the start, the trail crosses the Bull Springs Meadows at 9,500 feet.

To continue on to Apache Pass, turn left at the fence and enter the forest. Follow the trail an additional mile and a quarter to the pass. The total distance from the trailhead to the pass is between 3-1/2 to 4 miles, depending on the route. If you begin at the gate at the top of Palo Flechado pass, the hike will be about a mile shorter than the routes that begin at the trailhead at the bottom of the pass.

The sign at the trailhead offers some history, as well as maps and estimated distances. There is much helpful information on the sign, but it is hard to take it all in on a first visit. Another map can be found at www.angelfirefun.com.

History: The trail is named after Elliott S. Barker, who became the first game warden for the state of New Mexico in 1931 and served 22 years in that position. He was also a forest ranger and a supervisor. Barker is credited with finding a burned and orphaned bear cub in 1950 after a fire in the Lincoln National Forest. The bear cub was sent to the National Zoo in Washington D.C. and became "Smokey," the Forest Service's symbol of fire prevention. Barker wrote seven books based on his experiences in the outdoors and was a founding member of the National Wildlife Federation. He died in 1988 at the age of 101.

The same year a resident of Angel Fire, Kathy Kalen, began work to create a system of trails that would be easier to reach for those living there. Kalen says, "I volunteered at the Chamber. About 80 percent of our visitors asked, 'where are the hiking trails?' I would send them to Red River or Taos Ski area, as we did not have any trails. I thought to myself, we need trails here." She presented a recreation plan to the Carson National Forest for the current trails and formed the Moreno Valley Trekkers, the group that built the trails. The Trekkers began with a group of six members and has grown to 150. They built the trail to Apache Pass and beyond, over the course of several years, with the help of Volunteers for the Outdoors and the Forest Service.

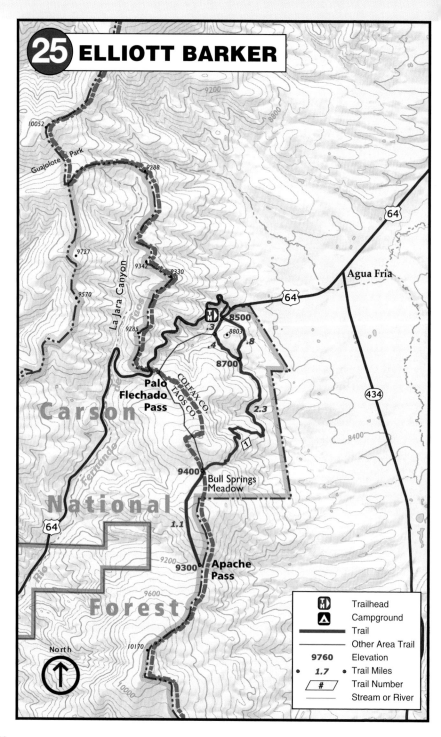

25 ELLIOTT BARKER

10052

Guajolote Park

9288

9727

9342

9330

La Jara Canyon

9570

9285

Taos

64

Agua Fria

64

8500

.3

8803

.8

.4

8700

434

COLFAX CO
TAOS CO.

Palo
Flechado
Pass

Carson

2.3

8400

1

Fernando

9400

Bull Springs
Meadow

National

64

1.1

Rio

9200

9300

Apache
Pass

9600

Forest

North

10170

10000

🚹	Trailhead
⛺	Campground
▬▬▬	Trail
────	Other Area Trail
9760	Elevation
• *1.7* •	Trail Miles
[#]	Trail Number
────	Stream or River

Hikes off of NM 518

The trails that follow are located off NM 518 south of Taos. These hikes are great to do in the fall. Aspens are found primarily above 9,000 feet, but the trees at higher elevations lose their leaves earlier in the fall. If you are hoping to find some aspen trees in full color by October, you might consider a drive out of Taos to the southeast. Amy Simms, recreation staff officer with the Carson National Forest says, "It is the perfect time to take advantage of the lower elevation hikes, where it is warmer and there are still some aspen leaves turning."

Drive south from the center of town to Ranchos de Taos and turn left onto NM 518. Leaving town, you gain altitude and at the top of the hill, there is a scenic overlook. You can look north toward Taos Mountain and El Salto and east to the rolling hills covered with evergreens and stands of aspen. As you pass the turn to Peñasco in the fall, there are flame-tinted yellow cottonwood trees in the Rio Pueblo drainage.

ASPENS ON COMALES

26. AMOLE CANYON TO GALLEGOS PEAK TRAIL (CNF #10 AND #182)

AMOLE CANYON

LENGTH: 4-miles roundtrip

DIFFICULTY: Moderate

ELEVATION: Begins at 8,300 feet; ends at 9,300 feet.

HIGHLIGHTS: Aspen groves, open meadows

DIRECTIONS: From Taos Plaza, head south 3 miles to NM 518. Turn left here and drive an additional 14 miles to reach the entrance to Amole Canyon on Forest Road 703. Drive a half-mile up a well-maintained dirt road, Forest Road 703 to the trailhead. The trip is 17.5 miles.

One of the closest hikes to Taos is Amole Canyon. Less than 30 minutes from the center of town, this area is best known for its winter cross country skiing. During other times of the year, Amole Canyon is usually quiet and lightly traveled. Park at the trailhead and cross the road to find the trail. Look for the second sign up the road that says #182. This is the beginning of the Amole Trail (#10) and Gallegos Peak Trail (#182). Climb up the trail through the aspen and mixed conifer forest. It is moderately steep here. After just under two miles, you reach the conjunction with the trail to Gallegos Peak (#182) turn right and head up a short, steep section until you reach the more level ridge that connects the trails in this area. Walk less than half a mile and you will see the place to the right where trail #7 Cañon Tio Maes meets #182. At several points throughout the hike, Forest Road 442 intersects with the trail to the north. To reach Gallegos Peak, continue along #182 another two miles. You will pass the conjunction with Gallegos Canyon Trail (#4) and Flechado Canyon Trail (#7) on the right. After this point, look out for a single trail section to the left that climbs up to the southside of Gallegos Peak and a meadow with views of the Jicarilla and Truchas Peaks.

Also accessible from the trailhead are a series of trails that make up the Amole Cross Country ski loop. The trails for these loops are across the road to the left. The lower trail follows the edge of the wooded area. Look for the trail signs and blue diamonds on the trees to help guide you. Cross the drainage in the first small meadow to reach a loop that goes through ponderosa pines. When the trail divides go right (east) for a short meander through the forest. If you haven't seen a trail arrow or blue diamond sign in a while, you may want to retrace your steps until you find one. A compass or GPS can be helpful in staying on the right track. There are often many bright blue Steller's jays here. After about 20 minutes on the trail, you will emerge into a meadow with a large stand of aspen trees. If you are hiking with smaller children, this would be a perfect location to end a short hike with a picnic.

For those interested in a longer hike, look for the trail markers and head northeast, staying to the right of the dry creek bed. Continue on until the trail widens out into a double-track section. After another 20 minutes you'll see a trail sign. Turn right into a large meadow and go up to the entry of the woods, the location of another large group of aspen trees – also a nice picnic spot. If you wish to continue, you can hike through the woods and find open areas with more stands of aspen trees. If you stay on the double-track section, you will shortly reach the intersection with Forest Road 422.

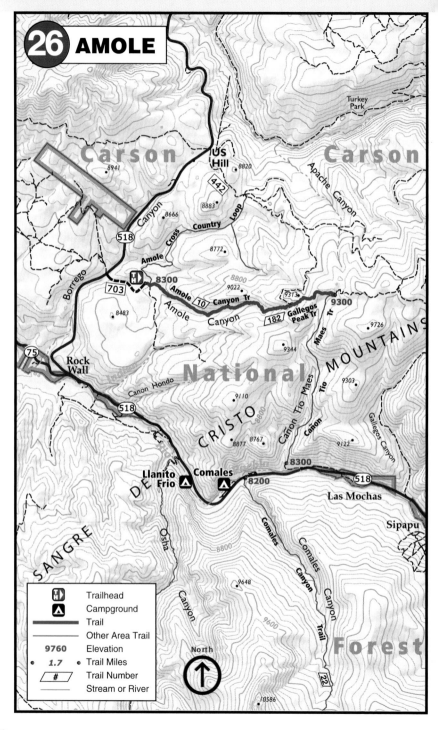

26 AMOLE

Turkey
Park

Carson   **Carson**

US
Hill

442

Country   Loop

518

Cross   Canyon

Amole

703   8300

Amole   10   Canyon Tr

182   Gallegos
Peak Tr

9300

Maes Tr

Borrego

Amole   Canyon

75

Rock
Wall

Canon Hondo

National   **MOUNTAINS**

Tio   Maes

518

CRISTO

Cañon Tio Maes

Cañon

Llanito
Frio   Comales   8300

8200

DE   Las Mochas

Sipapu

SANGRE   Osha

Comales

Comales   Canyon

Canyon

Canyon   Trail

Forest

8941
8820
8883
8666
8772
8800
9022
9313
8483
9726
9344
9303
9110
8800
8877   8767
9122
9648
9600
10586

	Trailhead
	Campground
───	Trail
───	Other Area Trail
9760	Elevation
● *1.7* ●	Trail Miles
#	Trail Number
	Stream or River

North

22

27. CAÑON TIO MAES TRAIL (CNF #5)

ASPEN FOREST

This trail follows a creek bed in a moderate-to-steep climb beginning at near 8,000 feet. I found a walking stick to be helpful in climbing and descending the steeper portions of the trail. Enter through a gate; you'll find the trail first crosses the creek bed and then becomes more rocky and steep. There are fir trees, scrub oak and aspen along the creek. After a bit of a climb, you'll arrive at a meadow to your left that is surrounded by aspen trees. Continue on the trail to a second aspen grove. The trail begins to flatten here and gradually becomes a deeply rutted double-track section. After more than an hour of climbing at about the 2-mile point, you will come to an open meadow, with views to the surrounding ridges. This makes a great place to rest or end the hike. If you continue farther north, you will reach the intersection with the Gallegos Peak Trail (CNF #182). Be aware that this trail does allow motorcycle access.

LENGTH: 4-miles roundtrip

DIFFICULTY: Moderate to difficult

ELEVATION: Begins at 8,300 feet; ridge at 9,300 feet

HIGHLIGHTS: Aspen stands

DIRECTIONS: From Taos Plaza, drive 3 miles and turn left on to NM 518. Continue on NM 518 past the turn to Peñasco. Go an additional 3 miles and look for the trail; turn after the second crossing of the Rio del Pueblo at mile marker 54. (The only visible sign faces the other direction.) Drive up a short paved section and park at the end. Follow a dirt road up the hill to the entry gate. The trip is about 22 miles and takes approximately 35-40 minutes from the center of town.

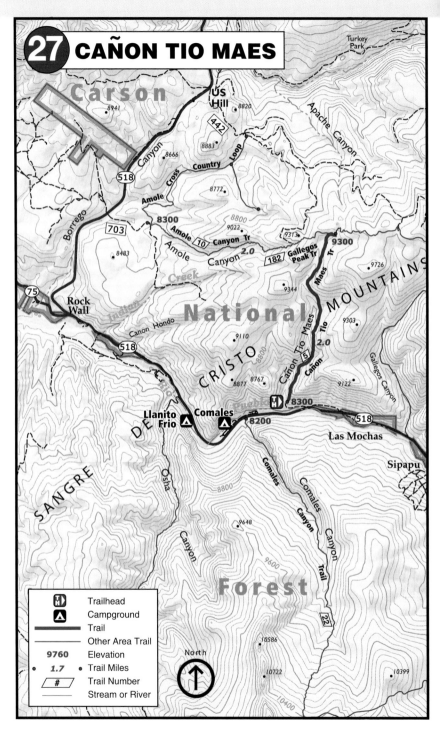

27 CAÑON TIO MAES

Carson

US Hill 8820

442

8883

Country

8941

8666

Cross

Amole

703

8300

Amole 10 Canyon Tr 2.0

Amole

8483

Canyon

Apache Canyon

Turkey Park

8772

8800

9022

9313

182 Gallegos Peak Tr

9300

9726

Borrego

75

Rock Wall

Indian

Creek

Canon Hondo

518

National

9110

8800

9344

Maes Tr

MOUNTAINS

9303

Cañon Tio Maes

2.0

Cañon

5

9122

Gallegos Canyon

CRISTO

8877 8767

Pueblo

Rio

Llanito Frio

Comales

8300

8200

518

Las Mochas

SANGRE

DE

Osha

Canyon

8800

9648

9600

Comales

Canyon

Comales

Canyon

Trail

22

Sipapu

Forest

10586

North

10722

10400

10399

Legend

🅷	Trailhead
⛺	Campground
────	Trail
────	Other Area Trail
9760	Elevation
• 1.7 •	Trail Miles
#	Trail Number
──	Stream or River

28. COMALES CANYON TRAIL (CNF #22)

HIKER ON COMALES CANYON TRAIL

LENGTH: 8-mile roundtrip

DIFFICULTY: Moderate to difficult, some steep sections

ELEVATION: 8,200 to 10,700 feet

HIGHLIGHTS: Follows a creek; aspen groves; fern-cover meadow; canyon rock walls

DIRECTIONS: From Taos Plaza, go south on Paseo del Pueblo Sur 3 miles. Turn left at NM 518 and go just over 15 miles to the intersection of NM 518 and NM 75 (to Peñasco). Stay on NM 518 for an additional 2.2 miles. Go past the Comales Campground to the left, around a curve. Immediately after the trail sign on the right, you can pull off or drive up a short four-wheel drive road to park at the trailhead. The whole drive from Taos Plaza to the trailhead is just over 20 miles.

Comales Canyon Trail begins on an open, rocky incline. The trail soon enters the woods and follows a creek. Surrounded by woods of aspen and pine trees, there are flowers, including monkshood and asters, to be seen in the summer and early fall. Rocky walls of orange and gray granite line the west side of the creek. There are numerous crossings with rocks and logs to provide a way across.

After about 50 minutes of gradual climbing, there is an aspen grove, which is a great destination or place to rest before resuming the hike. If you continue along the trail, you will reach the first meadow, after another 10 minutes. The meadow is followed by a second aspen grove. In this section, the trail levels out. As you continue further up, Comales will join the Cordova Canyon Trail, where there are views of the surrounding peaks, including Picuris Peak and Gallegos Peak.

If you head down the Cordova Canyon Trail, you will reach NM 518 at the Agua Piedra campground, more than 4 miles to the south of the Comales trailhead. You might choose to leave one car at the Agua Piedra campground and drive back to the Comales trailhead to begin the hike.

Comales continues farther up into the woods and eventually connects to several other trails including Osha Canyon Trail and Bear Mountain Trail.

During a fall hike, I saw a small black bear on the trail. The bear was meandering along, apparently in search of food and did not see my hiking partner and me. We had time to try to get a quick picture, and then we quietly and quickly returned down the trail. Our other option would have been to stop and let the bear escape into the woods before continuing on the trail.

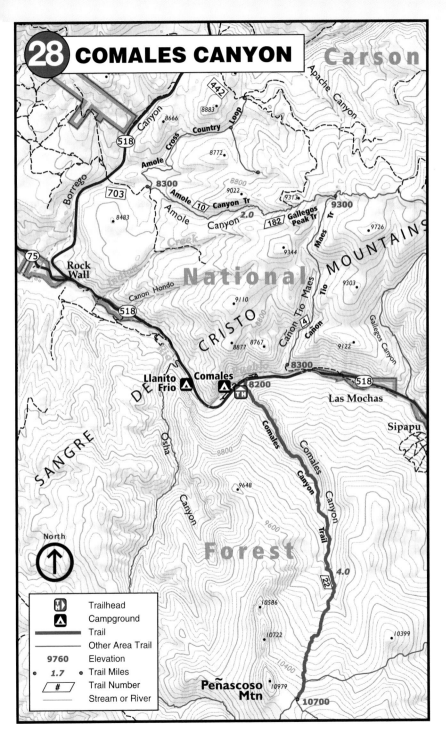

28 COMALES CANYON

Carson

Apache Canyon

442

8883

Canyon

8666

Cross

Country

Loop

518

8772

Amole

8800

703

8300

9022

Amole

10

Canyon Tr

9313

9300

8483

Amole

2.0

Canyon

182

Gallegos

Peak Tr

Maes Tr

9726

Creek

9344

National

Maes

9303

75

Rock
Wall

Canon Hondo

518

9110

Canon Tio Maes

Tio

CRISTO

8800

Cañon

9122

Cañon

8877

8767

Gallegos Canyon

8300

Comales

8200

518

Llanito
Frio

Comales

Las Mochas

DE

Osha

Comales

Sipapu

SANGRE

8800

Canyon

9648

Comales

Canyon

9600

Canyon

Trail

North

Forest

4.0

22

10586

10722

10399

10400

9760 — Elevation

Peñascoso
Mtn

10979

10700

🅷🅳	Trailhead
🅰	Campground
▬▬▬	Trail
─────	Other Area Trail
9760	Elevation
• 1.7 •	Trail Miles
#	Trail Number
─────	Stream or River

29. SERPENT LAKE (CNF #19)

SERPENT LAKE

LENGTH: About 7-miles roundtrip

DIFFICULTY: Moderate

ELEVATION: Begins at 10,300 feet; Serpent Lake at 11,800 feet

HIGHLIGHTS: Wildflowers during summer, blue alpine lake, views of Jicarita Peak

DIRECTIONS: From Taos Plaza, drive 3 miles south on Paseo del Pueblo to the intersection with NM 518. Turn left and continue southeast about 29 miles. From NM 518, turn right onto Forest Road 161. Go an additional 4 miles to trailhead. The forest road is dirt and there are some ruts on portions of the road, but it is generally passable by most vehicles. The trailhead, also known as Alamitos Trailhead, was improved recently to better accommodate horses on the trail.

Serpent Lake is a beautiful blue, high alpine lake surrounded by wildflowers and woods. It is located beneath treeless Jicarita Peak. Although not an easy hike, it is worth the moderate 3.5-mile climb to reach it. In the early summer, rains make this area south of Taos green and the trails wet; there may be some snow at higher elevations.

The Serpent Lake Trailhead is located at 10,300 feet and is reached by following NM 518 south of Taos to Forest Road 161. Serpent Lake Trail is part of a system called the Jicarita Peak Trails and is one of only three near Taos to be designated as a National Recreation Trail, which recognizes its local and regional significance. The other two trails are Columbine-Twining near Taos Ski Valley and the South Boundary Trail in Taos Canyon.

The Serpent Lake Trail begins with a gently rolling section of double track, going across a creek and some berms. It enters the woods and follows a series of switchbacks crossing a ditch and several small streams. The aspens are a glossy new green in the late spring, and a variety of birds can be heard singing. Francisco Cortez, the wildlife biologist with the Carson National Forest, says that the small gray pygmy nuthatch and the larger bluish Clark's nutcracker are among the most common birds to be seen in the fir and spruce forests. Cortez points out that larger birds such as the blue grouse and ptarmigan are also present here.

As the trail continues into the woods there is a stream to the left. When it runs full it creates a cascading waterfall. Look here for flowers such as blue columbine in late June and into July. After the crossing of Holman Ditch, there is a steeper rocky section up the hill through the woods. This part of the path may have water from melting snow and can be muddy in places. Hikers should proceed slowly, watching their footing on the wet rocks.

As the trail climbs higher, some areas of snow may remain early in the summer. Although there may be occasional drifts on the trail, it is usually passable. After more than 2 miles, the path crosses from the Carson National Forest into the Pecos Wilderness, which is indicated by a sign. The trail reaches a level section with larger rocks that leads to the turn for Serpent Lake, marked by a sign to the right. Turn here and go down the hill.

Stay left and above the marshy area at the base of the boulder field. Go an additional 0.3 miles to reach the gorgeous Serpent Lake area. Early in the summer wildflowers bloom here, including the white marsh marigold and yellow buttercup. Cross a series of stone steps that lead to the lake, located at 11,800 feet. Snowy Jicarita Peak, above the tree line at 12,835 feet, looms overhead. Although it can be windy at times, the lake is a beautiful place to have lunch. There is a smaller lake nearby and there are some campsites available. Watch for bighorn sheep and the yellow-bellied marmot, which are commonly seen in high alpine environments.

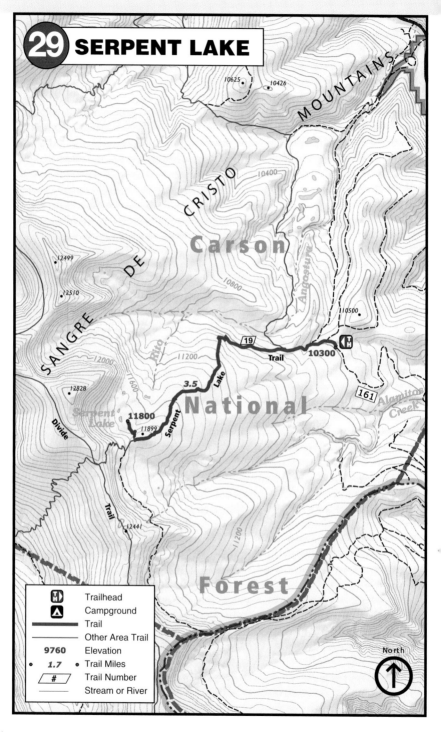

29 SERPENT LAKE

10625
10426

MOUNTAINS

CRISTO

10400

Carson

DE

12499

10800

12510

Angostura

110500

SANGRE

12000

11200

19

Rito

Trail

10300

11600

3.5

161

Alamitos Creek

12828

Serpent Lake

11800

Serpent Lake

National

11899

Divide

Serpent Lake

Trail

12441

11200

Forest

Trailhead
Campground
Trail
Other Area Trail
9760 Elevation
• *1.7* • Trail Miles
Trail Number
Stream or River

North

30. SANTA BARBARA (CNF #24 AND #25)

SANTA BARBARA ASPENS

LENGTH: 6- to 8-miles roundtrip to reach the meadows

DIFFICULTY: Mostly moderate

ELEVATION: 8,900 feet to approximately 9,700 feet

HIGHLIGHTS: Hike follows Rio Santa Barbara; possible wildlife sightings include wild turkey; aspens turning in the fall

DIRECTIONS: From Taos Plaza, drive 3 miles south on Paseo del Pueblo and turn left on NM 518. Climb US Hill and go a total of 16 miles before turning right on NM 75. Follow this road through Vadito and past the Camino Real Ranger District office. Shortly after the ranger office, turn left on to NM 73. Follow it for 1.5 miles, then turn left onto Santa Barbara Road and go another 5.5 miles to the Santa Barbara campground. Outside the campground, there is an outhouse and parking. There is a fee of $3 to park just outside the gate. If the campground is open, you can continue up the loop. It costs $8 to park here. The campground is closed at the end of September, and no fees are charged after it is closed. The outhouses remain open, but are not regularly maintained during the offseason.

The hike, designated #24 in the Carson National Forest, begins at the Santa Barbara campground located near Peñasco. It is located within the 223,000-acre Pecos Wilderness, which is part of both the Carson and the Santa Fe National Forests. The wilderness designation prohibits the use of any mechanized devices and ensures that hikers will encounter more undeveloped areas and opportunities for solitude.

Walk up through the campground about 0.3 a mile to the trailhead. Starting at approximately 8,800 feet in elevation, this hike follows the Rio Santa Barbara through mixed conifer and aspen forests. It begins with a gradual climb above the river and then drops down to join it. Here there are several small meadows that provide a great place to stop and rest. This part of the trail can be wet and there are often cows in the area.

The trail soon intersects with the Centennial Trail, which heads off to the right. Continue on the main trail and cross the bridge. The path climbs above the river. After about half a mile of moderate climbing, the trail divides. To follow trail #24, go up the hill to your left toward Pecos Falls. You will pass through stands of aspen. Rocky cliffs are visible across the river. Continue until you reach a gate. In this section, I saw a flock of wild turkeys. I surprised them on the trail and they scattered, some going up into the forest and others to the river below. One turkey took flight, spreading its enormous wings and tail. Male turkeys can weigh up to 21 pounds. Although wild turkeys were almost extinct in the U.S. in the early 1900s, the populations are stable or growing, according to the New Mexico Department of Game and Fish. Also in this section, I saw a blue grouse, several Steller's jays, and a hawk.

After passing through the gate, the trail continues a mild climb through more aspen. Follow this trail into an open meadow high above the river, which makes an excellent destination for a day hike.

Another option is to continue on the trail marked #25 at the dividing sign. You will encounter a series of beautiful meadows surrounded by aspen. The trail crosses the middle fork of the Rio Santa Barbara and leads to another group of meadows with views of Chimayosos Peak to the south. The path continues to both the Santa Barbara Divide and Truchas Lakes.

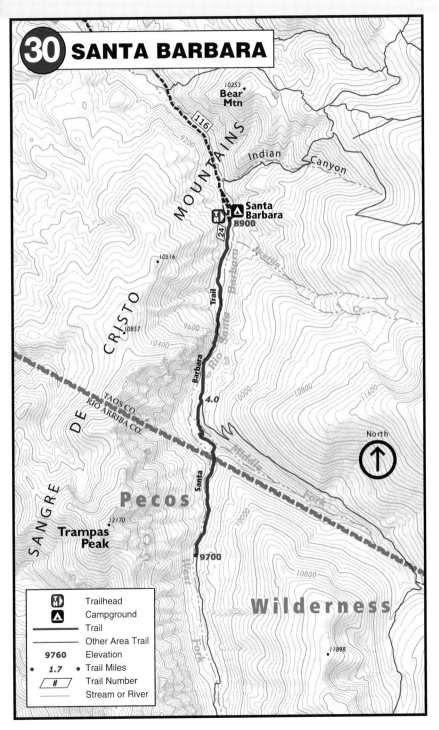

30 SANTA BARBARA

Bear Mtn
10253

116

9200

Indian Canyon

MOUNTAINS

Santa Barbara
8900

24

10516

Trail

Barbara

Rio Santa Barbara

Jicarita

10857

9600

10400

CRISTO

Barbara

4.0

10000

10800

11600

North
↑

Santa

Middle Fork

TAOS CO.
RIO ARRIBA CO.

RIO

DE

SANGRE

Pecos

Trampas Peak
12170

10000

West Fork

9700

10800

11898

Wilderness

🅷	Trailhead
⬛	Campground
——	Trail
	Other Area Trail
9760	Elevation
• **1.7** •	Trail Miles
#	Trail Number
	Stream or River

Near Taos

POSI PUEBLO
AT OJO CALIENTE

Ojo Caliente is located 42 miles southwest of Taos. The Posi Pueblo hike begins at the Ojo Caliente Mineral Springs.

POSI PUEBLO TRAIL

31. POSI PUEBLO

POTTERY SHARDS AT POSI PUEBLO RUINS

LENGTH: 2-miles

DIFFICULTY: Moderate with a short steep section at the beginning, uphill to the mesa

ELEVATION: Approximately 6,000 feet at the beginning, climbs over 380 feet

HIGHLIGHTS: Site of former pueblo, pottery shards

DIRECTIONS: Beginning at Taos Plaza, travel 4 miles north on Paseo del Pueblo Norte. At the intersection of US 64 and Highway 150 (Ski Valley Road) turn left (west) and drive for 7 miles. After crossing the Rio Grande Gorge Bridge, travel less than a mile and turn left at the West Rim Road. Drive another 8 miles with the gorge to your left. Turn right onto Highway 567 and go 9 miles. You will pass through the small town of Carson and arrive at the intersection with US 285. Turn left for the final 10 miles to Ojo. After passing El Rito (look for the sign that says "Pigs"), turn right at NM 414. You will go by several bed and breakfasts and the Ojo Caliente Fire Station before arriving at the entrance to the mineral springs.

There are several hikes that start at Ojo Caliente Mineral Springs. A hike and a soak make for a wonderful day trip only 45 minutes away from Taos. One of the most popular hikes is the 2-mile loop through the site of the ruins of the Posi-Ouinge (Posi) Pueblo.

You can pick up a trail map and brochure at the desk inside Ojo Caliente. The brochure, provided by the Bureau of Land Management (BLM) has some helpful drawings that help you imagine how the area may have looked in the past when it was inhabited by early Tewa people. The site was inhabited between approximately 1,300 and 1,400s CE and had thousands of rooms. Due to exposure to the elements, the adobe walls have disintegrated or melted over time, leaving mounds of land covered with pottery shards.

The hike begins with a moderately steep, rocky section. It is well-marked, and there are generally a few other people on the trail. You'll see some of the pink granite rock that defines the area. The hike levels out and goes through some rolling terrain and a dry wash. Rock piles have been formed into sculptures in the wash.

After about 15 minutes, you'll encounter a fence with an opening and a place to sign in. Continue on the trail, which is surrounded by cactus, sage, and juniper. There is not much shade on the trail, and it can be breezy at times.

As you reach the flat mesa, you will notice quartz and sparkling mica-specked rocks. There are shards of pottery scattered across the site of the Posi village, some of the shards arranged in groups around rocks. You can envision a whole pot from the small pieces that contain bits of patterns and decoration. According to Paul Williams, archeologist with the BLM, it is fine to pick up the pottery shards, but you should replace the pieces in the places you found them.

There are many side trails on the plateau, and it is pleasant to wander up over the mounds and arroyos until you reach the overlook of the Rio Ojo Caliente. It is easy to become a bit disoriented, but hard to become very lost. The whole hike, including some wandering, can be done in an hour to an hour and a half.

The Posi Pueblo: Williams says that Posi was one of seven Pueblos along the Ojo Caliente during the 1,300 and 1,400s CE. It is estimated that as many as 10,000 people lived in these pueblos. Williams says that there were 2,000 to 3,000 rooms built up to three-stories tall at Posi, using courses of adobe mud. This pueblo was built using the same methods as those used at the Taos Pueblo. At its peak, this site was so large that the largest settlement at Chaco Canyon, if picked up and set at Posi, would fit into the plaza area. Williams says that the region was extensively farmed using terrace gardens and the rich riverbed area to grow corn, beans, squash, and cotton.

The Posi Pueblo is believed to be one of the most important Tewa settlements. In the oral history of the Tewa people, Posi is where two groups came together – the Summer People and the Winter People – to build Posi, which is also called "The Greenness Pueblo." It was their home for two centuries, until something – perhaps an epidemic – came upon the people and a decision was made to leave and to build other villages.

Williams reminds visitors: "For the Tewa people, this is not a ruin or even abandoned. It is full of the spirit of the people who lived there. It continues to be an important site. Out of respect for the past, don't take pottery shards or other artifacts. The pueblo is returning to the earth, as the Tewa people desire, and we don't need to hurry or disturb the process."

Mineral Spring Resort and Spa: Ojo Caliente is a favorite destination for locals and visitors. The mineral springs provide healing waters for people today, just as they did for the Tewa people. There are 10 mineral pools, with temperatures varying from approximately 86 to 107 degrees. Spa treatments, a restaurant, and overnight lodging are available. Regardless of when you visit, the pools at Ojo provide a great way to relax. A weekday visit will likely be the most calming, but even on a busy weekend, you can find a quiet corner. There is one large oval pool at approximately 86 degrees that is great for swimming. The other pools are warmer, with the Arsenic pool being the hottest at up to 107 degrees.

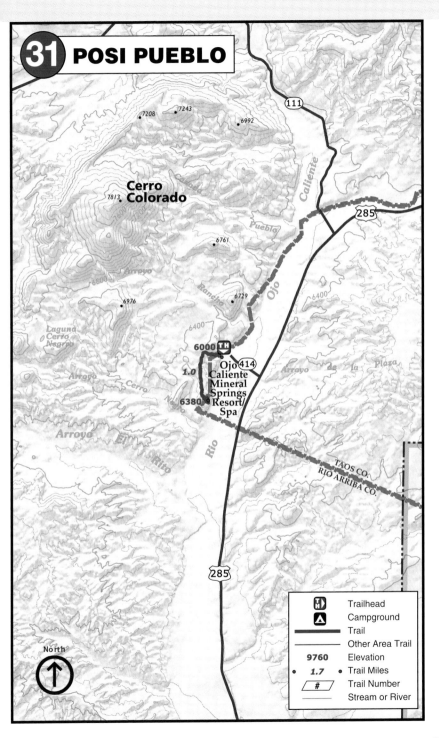

31 POSI PUEBLO

111

Cerro
Colorado
7813

7208
7243
6992

6761

Pueblo

Rancho
6729

Ojo

Caliente

285

6400

6976

6000

Laguna
Cerro
Negro

6400

1.0

Ojo 414
Caliente
Mineral
Springs
Resort
Spa

6380

Arroyo de la Plaza

Arroyo Cerro

Arroyo El

Rio

TAOS CO.
RIO ARRIBA CO.

285

North

	Trailhead
	Campground
	Trail
	Other Area Trail
9760	Elevation
• *1.7* •	Trail Miles
#	Trail Number
	Stream or River

Appendix A

LOCAL OUTFITTERS AND RESOURCES

Mudd-n-Flood on Bent Street (575) 751-9100

Taos Mountain Outfitters on the Plaza (575) 758-9292

Cottam's mid-town location near McDonalds on Paseo del Pueblo Sur (575) 758-8719

Taos Herb – 710 Paseo del Pueblo Sur (575) 758-1991

Cid's Food Market – 623 Paseo del Pueblo Norte (575) 758-1148

Taos Native Plant Society – website: www.npsnm.org

Taos Visitor Center is on the south side of town at 1139 Paseo del Pueblo Sur (575) 758-3873. An entire room is devoted to hiking trails and maps, and staff can answer your questions about current weather patterns.

Carson National Forest has an office at 208 Cruz Alta Road (575) 758-6200 with lots of maps and can provide more information about trail conditions. Website: www.fs.usda.gov/carson/.

Bureau of Land Management (BLM) Taos Field office is at 226 Cruz Alta Road (575) 758-8851. They are a good resource for planning hikes on BLM land. Website: www.blm.gov/nm/st/en.html.

Wild Rivers Visitor Center is located north of Questa (575) 586-1150. Here you can find information about a variety of spectacular trails that take you down to the Rio Grande.

Rio Grande Gorge Visitor Center is located about 30 minutes south of town near Pilar (575) 751-4899. Maps, books, and friendly staff can help guide you to hiking and camping.

Appendix B

WILDFLOWERS AND A MUSHROOM

Middle to late summer is usually the best time to see wildflowers in the high country. Local naturalist David Witt says that the Hondo Valley and the Wheeler Wilderness have received attention from botanists, due to the extensive number of flowers and plants in the area. Witt has compiled a list of plants found locally, which has 320 species listed. "This little patch of ground is remarkably diverse," he says. Witt leads hikes for the Taos Native Plant Society. Usually the groups see many wildflowers and sometimes the Amanita muscaria, a poisonous mushroom. This reddish, speckled, often dome-shaped mushroom looks like something from a fairy tale and shouldn't be eaten. Witt says, "The late season highlight of the high country is the gentians…look for the Parry Gentian. It lives in the forest edges around Williams Lake and is beautiful, dark blue cup shape." He adds, "Flora admirers should look at and photograph wildflowers, but not pick them. The plants put all their energy into seed production to create the next generation and should not be disturbed."

There are small, portable flower guides available at local outfitters, but here are a few flowers to be on the lookout for:

WILDFLOWER DESCRIPTIONS

AMANITA MUSCARIA

Amanita Muscaria

BLUE COLUMBINE

Blue Columbine
- Large, dramatic white and blue petaled flowers
- July to August
- Moist open areas, aspen groves, rocky slopes

TANSY ASTER

Tansy Aster
- Thin purple petals with yellow centers
- June to August
- Along creeks and streams

FIREWEED

Fireweed
- Purplish-red flowers on a tall stem
- July and August
- Open areas, disturbed land
- The first flower to appear after a fire

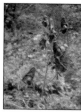

MONKSHOOD

Monkshood
- Dark purple petals that fold back on each other on a tall stem
- June to August
- Near streams and other wet areas

MOUNTAIN HARE-
BELL / BELLFLOWER

Mountain Harebell/Bellflower
- Delicate purple bells on a tall stem
- June to September
- Meadows, forest clearings

NODDING ONION

Nodding Onion
- Pink balls made of six tiny petals hanging from top of stem
- June to September
- Open meadows, moist areas

SCARLET PAINT-
BRUSH

Scarlet Paintbrush
- Big red spikes atop a sturdy stem
- June to August
- Meadows and hillsides

SCARLET GILIA FAIRY
TRUMPET

Scarlet Gilia Fairy Trumpet
- Bright red-orange flowers shaped like small trumpets
- July to September
- Open dry areas

TALL CONEFLOWER

Tall Coneflower
- Large yellow flowers with petals that droop away from protruding center
- June to August
- Moist meadows and streams

WILD BERGAMOT

Wild Bergamot
- Grouping of narrow purple petals centered on top of a square stem
- June to August
- Dry areas near trail

TALL CHIMING BELLS

Tall Chiming Bells
- Light blue, bell-shaped flowers
- June to August
- Near creeks

Index

PHOTO BY JOE JATCKO

CINDY BROWN WITH DENNIS

About the Author

Cindy Brown is the hiking columnist for *The Taos News*. She is the author of *Lessons from Nature in Healing, Strength and Flexibility*, along with hiking guides for bed and breakfasts. She wrote "Hiking Tips for Visitors" for the final edition of *Day Hikes in the Taos Area* by Kay Matthews. Her nature photos were shown in the 2014-2015 "Ah, Wilderness" exhibit at Taos Town Hall. Her business, Two Meadows Coaching, provides assistance to people making life transitions.